"When we were children we had dreams, we had hope. As we grow older we lose something significant, something magical... actually we don't lose this, it's taken from us."

"We have a voice so that we may speak, and we speak to be heard. Since our words have the power to change the world then let's practice speaking on something worth hearing about... I've learned to never underestimate an ideology; the largest threat to our world today is a dangerous ideology. To win a war we need to understand the foundation their beliefs were built upon. No amount of money, weapons, or number of soldiers will prevail against a dangerous idea... We have to be able to change minds."

L.L Brunk

"We didn't know enough and we still don't know enough... Most of us - me included - had a very superficial understanding of the situation and history, and we had a frighteningly simplistic view of recent history, the last 50 years..." Lacking the knowledge to achieve a successful end...

General Stanley McChrystal

Discovering Purpose

L.L Brunk

A Military Vets Memoirs'

Before heading to a warzone there were rational answers to be found, and hope was prevalent. I recognized that to hold a grudge against those who've wronged me doesn't hurt anyone but me... Frankly they were not worth the stress...

Grasping Forgiveness

Not long ago in the Freudian nomenclature the term forgiveness would seem out of place, but in recent years psychology has been changing, and how we view forgiveness is an interesting example of that change. A number of psychologists now argue that healing of such wounds as child abuse for example is impossible as long as the victim is unwilling to forgive. 1(M. Scott Peck; psychologist) A case in point of a victim who was at one time unwilling to forgive, or unable to, is Simon Wiesenthal, the author of 2 The Sunflower, On the Possibilities and Limits of Forgiveness.

Wiesenthal is a Jew who was imprisoned in a Nazi concentration camp during World War II. One day he was taken from his work and brought by a nurse to the bedside of a dying SS member. The murderer wanted to confess all of his crimes and obtain absolution from a Jew, and the nurse was asked to bring him one, any Jew, Simon was chosen.

After the desperate dying SS member speaks to Wiesenthal about all of the horrible things he's done to the Jewish people, and he confesses he regrets doing, he begs Simon for forgiveness, not knowing who he was. Knowing he was a Jew was all that mattered then. Faced with his choices Wiesenthal chooses to leave the SS members bedside without speaking. The SS member begged, and he did not try to justify his crimes, knowing that he deserved death, but Wiesenthal never said a word to him. Should this murderer have been forgiven? He certainly did not deserve compassion, or mercy, for these would never be granted from an SS member to a Jew.

Though it may be difficult, depending on our different circumstances, we should still try to grasp how necessary and liberating forgiveness can be, even for Wiesenthal when faced with the dying SS member, who murdered women and children. Being unforgivable enslaves the one who can't forgive, and this conceives hate, where there is never any justice.

We must remember that murderers were not born as so, and Wiesenthal explains this well in his own words. Years later, after the war had ended, Wiesenthal spoke to the SS members' mother, where he learned that his name was Karl. Wiesenthal writes, 3 "Karl had certainly been a 'good boy. But a graceless period of his life had turned him into a murderer." (Sunflower 95) Lower on this same page he wrote, "I reflect that people like him are still being born, people who can be indoctrinated with evil."

When someone is so full of hate, one cannot expect that they will accept any ones forgiveness, because their hearts have grown so cold. Is there a possibility that the most evil of people can be forgiven? Is it even right to grant forgiveness to Karl, even if he did confess that he was wrong and sorry for the horrible crimes that he committed? We see when reading The Sunflower (54-55) that the sorrow Karl felt was genuine and he would never be able to forgive himself. So should Wiesenthal have had mercy, and told this man that he does not resent him anymore, and that although Karl is guilty of being a horrible person, he does not detest him? The killer would still have to live his few remaining days in misery over the horrible crimes he had committed, having nightmares till he took his last breath. There are people who would say that this punishment is enough. Why would Wiesenthal hold onto this hate anyway? Does he want his inner wounds to continue hurting? Does he want to remain a victim? If he desires healing, the only way to receive this would be by forgiving. But how can he forgive such a man, who slaughtered his people and tortured them?

Harold S. Kushner is Rabbi Laureate of Temple Israel in Natrick, Massachusetts. He is also an author. His comments about forgiveness directed to The Sunflower are very influential. He says, "Forgiving is not something we do for another person, as the Nazi asked Wiesenthal to do for him. Forgiving happens inside us. It represents a letting go of the sense of grievance, and perhaps most importantly a letting go of the role of victim. For a Jew to forgive the Nazis would not mean, God forbid, saying to them 'What you did was understandable, I can understand what led you to do it and I don't hate you for it.' It would mean saying 'What you did was thoroughly despicable and puts you outside the category of decent human beings. But I refuse to give you the power to define me as a victim. I refuse to let your blind hatred define the shape and content of my Jewishness. I don't hate you; I reject you.' And then the Nazi would remain chained to his past and to his conscience, but the Jew would be free." Kushner has the right idea.

Is there a time where to forgive someone might be wrong? Some people would say yes, forgiveness can be wrong. This is how Maj. Gen. U.S Army Officer, Sidney Shachnow felt after he read The Sunflower. He says, "Simon Wiesenthal was right in not granting forgiveness, for two reasons. First, he did not have the moral right to do so, and second this savage did not deserve it. He stepped over the boundary where forgiveness is possible. That SS officer should take up his case with God. I personally think he should go to hell and rot there. I doubt very much that my God would grant him forgiveness. After all, what does it take to serve in hell?" (243) People like General Shachnow, who say forgiveness can be wrong, are they not people who try to justify their hate? When you don't forgive someone, doesn't this mean you resent what they've done to you? The unforgiven is obviously regarded with strong ill will, and this defines hate, so when you resent someone this means you hate them also. And when you hate someone you are a murderer in a "sense", because in your heart the one you hate, and choose to resent is dead to you. There is no justifying the crimes of the SS member Karl, who sought after forgiveness from Wiesenthal, but is there a just reason that Wiesenthal had not to forgive this man? The definition for just is being right in law and ethics, fair minded, and having good intention. In a world where violence seems to be ever increasing, can any person truly afford to hate or not forgive anybody?

Is there a just reason to forgive Karl, or any killer Nazis? Is there a possibility of unity between a Nazi and a Jew? Certainly not, because a Nazi hates a Jew, and a Jew can never trust a Nazi. Just perhaps though, an unjust treated man can accept an apology from a sincerely sorry man, who is on his death bed. There's no doubt that many Germans' encouraged hate towards the Jews' during World

War II, especially the SS members of the Nazi Party, of whom Karl was a part of. 6 On August 15, 1935, in Berlin thousands of Germans gathered at a mass rally in order to listen to anti-Semitic speeches and to hear of a future Germany cleansed of Jews. There were two banners that read: "The Jews Are Our Misfortune" and "Women and girls, the Jews are your ruin." (Daniel Jonah Goldhagen) The Jews were not even slaves in the traditional manner, because slaves are not supposed to be socially dead, they are depended on for production and even honor. (Daniel Jonah Goldhagen, Hitler's Willing Executioners 168-169) Many times slaves lived within society, and had social relations and ties to the oppressors. There is certainty that to the majority of Germans, the Jews were socially dead. All they wanted from the Jews was their suffering and death; there was no other purpose for them. These Germans were so prideful that they thought of themselves as the ultimate race, and their arrogance and longing for power caused many of them to become evil. They believed that they were super humans, perhaps like Greek gods of mythology. The Greek gods who were selfish beings that used humanity for basically entertainment, and usually cared very little about their problems, because the humans were not comparable to them; In this way many Germans were trying to brainwash their fellows into believing that other human beings apart from them were of little importance when compared to the German race. And the Jews were thought of as sub humans. The Nazis during World War II, were worse than the gods of Greek mythology because they planned on being rid of all other perceived lesser races of human beings, starting with the Jews. 8 Their ideology claimed that members of the master race could be created in a methodical way, and could just as easily advocate the methodical extermination of all lesser races. There was a pamphlet put out by the SS command that described the Jew in these words: "From a biological point of view he seems completely normal. He has hands and feet and a sort of brain. He has eyes and a mouth. But, in fact, he is a completely different creature, a horror. He only looks human, with a human face, but his spirit is lower than that of an animal. A terrible chaos runs rampant in this creature, an awful urge for destruction, primitive desires, unparalleled evil, a monster, and subhuman." (Tom Segev, Soldiers of Evil 80-81) Can a German, who believes like this, be forgiven by a Jew, who they don't even consider to be human? If these SS members think that they are super humans, then why would they ever accept forgiveness from a petty creature that is less than an animal? It seems that the only way an SS soldier would even ask for forgiveness from a Jew is if he realized that his beliefs about them were wrong. The SS member would have to be convinced that Jews were human beings, not less than animals, but equal to a German, before he could ask a Jew for forgiveness.

The apology would have to be man to man, not Nazi to a Jew, or a god to a creature. When Karl confessed his crimes to Wiesenthal, and sought after his forgiveness, what he was saying was, "I am not better than you, and I am guilty of killing innocent human beings, not creatures of horror full of unparalleled evil." In fact the realization that Karl came to while he was dying in misery was that he was the different creature, a horror with a human face, with a terrible chaos running rampant inside him. He was the monster and subhuman, not the Jews. It's truly ironic that when Karl begged Wiesenthal to forgive him, he knew that he was the one who was less human then the Jew. So the position Wiesenthal was truly in was that he had his enemy dying before him, and admitting that he was not superior in any way to a Jew. This enemy gave Wiesenthal a respect that was unimaginable coming from a Nazi directed to a Jew. He needed something desperately from someone his peers would consider to be a worthless creature, but who Karl now saw as a savior. The enemies pride was gone and he knew that he was going to die a worthless creature of destruction and death. Imagine a Greek god asking a human being to forgive him of his sins, and confessing to this man that he was worthless in his sight, hardly comparable to the greatness of a human, because a human has a soul. Well, Karl may have felt like he gained much when he first put on his SS uniform, but what did this profit him, if he traded his soul? He was dying with nothing, so in knowing this why couldn't Wiesenthal be the better "person" and grant him forgiveness in the proper manner? Perhaps he could have said, "You are not even worth hating, for you have ruined yourself, and you will die knowing that you were a killer for Hitler, nothing more. So, I truly pity you and I am sorry for you. Because although you will be buried with family and friends mourning over you, and a beautiful sunflower will be planted over your grave, you will still die knowing that you chose to be a murderer, and a monster. I will probably leave with a painful death and be buried in a shallow grave along with the rest of my people, and no person will care or remember us, but at least I will die knowing I am a man, and not a monster. I cannot speak on behalf of all the other Jews, whom you have murdered or made to suffer, and there is no justifying your crimes to them, but I forgive you for the pain you've caused me. I will no longer allow myself to be emotionally affected by you, or any other member of the SS. I choose to not hate you, because I see you as a pitiful creature that has nothing to hope for, and this is how I would have seen you if you were still killing us in your SS uniform. You were not only blind, and a lost child, but you were already dead years ago. Because you see, when you chose to join the SS Nazis you gave your life and soul to Hitler, and he used your members to do his bidding. Every time you took a life you lost more of your own, and you lost more of your soul, because you were constantly giving more of yourself to Hitler's will. My life has never really been taken, nor will it ever be, for I do not hand over my life to anyone in regards to what I know is morally wrong and damaging to my soul. However when I leave this world, I believe I will die in peace now. Thanks for showing me that there is still hope for humanity, and unity, even between a monster and a man, or even a German and a Jew. Goodbye now."

Could Wiesenthal have rightly forgiven the SS member Karl? Whether, or not he could have is irrelevant now. People have had much time to think about this situation that Wiesenthal was in, and meditate on the choices that could have been made in the room where the dying SS member laid. We must not forget though that Wiesenthal was the one who truly faced the mire and torture that these SS members had put people through. We could never truly know what we would have done, or said, if we were in Wiesenthal's place. There is certainty though that he didn't make a wrong choice by keeping silent, because his response to Karl, or lack thereof, was left open for interpretation, and Karl took his last breath knowing that a Jew had listened to his confession. Karl knew this man left knowing in his heart that the apology he heard was sincere, and this is well enough. If we are grasping for an understanding of forgiveness, remember the question that we can be thankful Wiesenthal has left for us. We can ask ourselves, "What would I have done?" Perhaps there should now be another question you have after reading this, "Can you truly justify a reason to hate, or not forgive anybody?"

A child was born, a lovely little girl, and a father had to find a better way to provide for her in a failing economy. I joined the service and deployed soon after. Having never left the comfort of my home nation, culture shock was inevitable.

I Hate Having To Wait In Kuwait

A soldier's account of a hellish time spent in a waste land that serves no other purpose but to make one suffer. Leaving you thankful for the life you have outside of her clutches.

On the bus ride from the barren ghost town airport to the military post there are shadows seen in the moonlight, rising out from the desert. Large chunks of medal, stone, road kill and lots of garbage sticking out of the sand to the left and right of the street our cramped full bus drives down. I don't believe the occasional road kill I saw was killed by any vehicle at all because the carcasses didn't have any severe damage. You see this is not the kind of road kill you may be accustomed to seeing in America. These are not cats, raccoons, skunks, dear, or even dogs you see laying dead on the side of the road. In Kuwait you see only dead horses, to the left and right you'll see dead horses, large rotting carcasses. I probably saw more than seven dead horses during the forty minute bus ride to the military post in Kuwait. It was as if they were not allowed to go beyond the borders, and when they tried they died, now casting their own shadows as a warning for anyone who would ever dare wander into the vast desert.

I hate having to wait in Kuwait...

I can swear this place is one of Dante's floors of Hell that the living has to pass through before we get to the cradle of life, the fallen Eden-Iraq (which isn't very nice either). I suppose the thought may just be a romantic notion, but I also felt like Kuwait may be on the outskirts of Gods' canvas, the edges of this painting called Earth. When first getting off of the plane and stepping out into the desert air of the waste land the first thought is shit. Because this is what you smell, a gust of shitty night air blowing into your face. Not really gag inducing, but just bad enough to leave you feeling like you want to pass through this place as quickly as possible, but that's the joke really, for Kuwait never lets you pass through fast enough, and the smell of defecation always lingers in your nostrils. I can't judge the people here, have not met enough of them, but I feel sorry for the heat they have to deal with daily.

What was most impressive though, almost like an unexpected gust of refreshing cool air on a scorching hot day, was the sight of the rising sun on the horizon of this apocalyptic looking desert. I have taken pictures of the rising sun but when I look at the images the feeling is not the same. There was this feeling of gratitude followed by sadness when I first saw the sun emerge. Never could I imagine a time when I would be able to look at the sun without having to turn away, and I was truly in awe of the blood red orb that I could stare at without blinking. She spoke and she said, "I still see you Eden, I see what you were and I remember, so in your memory I will bring beauty back to you for these morning moments." And later I learned that when she left she shined her beauty kindly when she wished the dead land a restful night. The sunset and the sunrise is the only beauty on this floor of Hell we call Kuwait, and the sight is not the same anywhere else. The hours in between the sunrise and sunset our so horrific that during those hours you'll forget her rising and setting beauty, and you'll remember all too well the Hell you're in.

As I said earlier Kuwait does not let you leave as quickly as you will, she makes you suffer some, almost to the point where you can take no more. In the day she beats down on you, and the (at first glance) glorious sun turns into a monster just when you were foolish enough to reach out your hand towards her beauty. She changes as soon as she fully emerges from the horizon; she is possessed, becoming something else, the tone changes from a peace like a bubbling brook to an ear piercing shriek. She snaps out at you and you try to pull back, but it's too late.

You are told that you will only be in her land for a few hours, and then you will catch a flight to Iraq, but she changes her mind and keeps you for a day. When the morning comes you feel that peace again from the rising sun, causing you to once again fall for her seduction, and you know that you will be heading out that day, for surely plans won't change again. But as soon as the sun fully emerges you somehow know that you will not be leaving yet, you have not suffered enough.

Somehow your bags are loaded on a plane that you cannot yet board. Your clothes, your hygiene bag and even your book-to read and escape in some way from the Hell you are in, are all packed on a plane that seems to be going nowhere soon.

The heat is so horrible that your mind feels dull, your senses weak. You feel helpless to defend yourself, and to even reach some water or food seems like a chore as you walk towards your sustenance. You feel grimy, so damp with funk, and you realize that you are contributing to that rancid smell you first noticed when you stepped off of the plane.

Four days went by in Kuwait like groundhogs day, one could not tell if it was four days, or four weeks. And the schedule for our departure kept on changing, so by the time we were on the bus heading towards our flight out to Iraq we felt too weak, and too battered to be joyful. I personally felt violated, like I wanted to huddle into a corner on the bus and try to find some peace in sleep. This is what she waits for of course, she is waiting for you to break, for you to surrender. And then she lets you go with her mark, she releases you, and from now on you will appreciate your life a little bit more where ever you are, being thankful that you are no longer in Kuwait.

On the flight out of Kuwait this soldier feels relieved that he is heading to a war zone like Iraq where at least he will have a purpose. This is how much I hate Kuwait.

The many life lessons a year deployed to Iraq reaps... There is corruption everywhere and in every organization, but there are those with honor also.

Army Article-The First and The Last

The focus of this article is to remind leaders in the Army of their responsibilities. This article is also meant to show people some of the silly drama that happens in the life of a soldier who works on the personnel side of the house. There is much good that is done in the Army, but there is also much more that could be done. Hopefully this article will inspire the right people to step up, for this is the primary purpose of this piece.

"No one is more professional than I. I am a Noncommissioned Officer, a leader of soldiers...I know my soldiers and will 'always' place their needs "above my own"...I will communicate consistently with my soldiers and "never" leave them "uninformed..."

From the Creed of the Non Commissioned Officer

Many soldiers join the military for many reasons, and as a soldier I will tell you that most of the reasons I've observed are not patriotic.

When I first joined the Army I joined because I had a daughter to support and the economy was going down the drain. I needed stability in my life, and assurance that my family's needs would be met. I was desperate, and the best possible life for my children is always the utmost on my list of priorities. My daughter needed financial, and more importantly, medical support, so I decided to join the armed forces to provide for my child all that I felt she needed.

When I first spoke with the Army Recruiter, (Air Force people were out on a late lunch that day), I told him I didn't want to be an infantry man. I told him my reasons for wanting to join, and then I asked him if there were any job offers in the Army for a Human Resource Specialist. I also asked him if it was at all possible to have a job that was less likely to deploy than others. (I didn't want to leave my daughter for long if this could at all be avoided.) The recruiter told me that the job I was asking about was the least likely to deploy to Iraq. He went on to tell me that I would be provided with housing for my family, college paid for, the best medical and financial means, and that I would be working nine to five just like any civilian job. I was sold... I was young. I was naive.

I was placed in the delayed entry program; five times a week I would run with my Army Recruiter and he would do pushups and set ups with me, but I did not yet have to leave my family for BASIC. The Army Recruiter seemed motivated to better prepare me for BASIC, and he was trying to inspire me. He seemed like a nice guy, and we even had a barbecue with our families together. All in all my first opinion of the Army was, 'this is a family', and I felt secure.

Was at BASIC Training when my wife, (at that time), decided she didn't want to be with me anymore, for I was taking too long to grow up. She was keeping in contact with my Army recruiter, and I was bothered by the way the recruiter was handling her. He was leaving her misinformed on many things. One of the biggest lies, from my Recruiter to my wife, was that she would continue to receive the California housing rate from me if she chose to stay there, (regardless of wherever I was going to be stationed after BASIC). He led her to believe that she would get loads of money from me, and he encouraged her to separate from me. I won't go much more into this, but I will just say that my time in BASIC was extra strenuous because of what was happening back home. I was fearful of losing my family and this was always on my mind throughout my training. After BASIC, when I was stationed in Fort Riley Kansas, I would have never guessed the lessons I would need to learn fast.

My first job in the Army was working in a Detachment of the First Cavalry Division; in-processing soldiers fresh out of BASIC. I was the one who welcomed the new soldiers to the base, and I handled all of their important paperwork. I signed them onto the post and made sure important documents like their life insurance was done properly. I would listen to their reasons for joining as I was signing multiple documents. I asked every soldier I in-processed why they joined, (this was my conversation starter to help the time go by as I filled out their required forms.)

You may be surprised to know the response I received by most when I asked the infantry soldiers why they joined. Quite simply they would say, "I just want to know what it feels like to kill a person." Perhaps you are not as naïve as I was at that time, and this news doesn't surprise you at all, but I-sure as the Pope isn't Muslim-was very surprised indeed by their response. Multiple soldiers said this same thing with maybe a slight difference in the wording; "I just want to know what it feels like to kill somebody," or, "Um, I don't know man... I just want to feel what it's like to waste a terrorist," or "I've wondered what it feels like to kill somebody, and now I'll get my chance," and a few other quotes. It all meant basically the same thing, they wanted to kill, and not get in trouble for doing so.

Now know and understand, not every single infantry soldier I in-processed responded in the same way. There were a smaller amount of infantrymen who would say things like, "I am very patriotic and I want to serve my country," or "My father was a soldier and I want to make him proud," or they would say something in reference to 911. "After they attacked us I was so angry that I felt like I had to do something," or "I felt that I had to do my part for my country; for our freedom." There was a couple times infantrymen would even say, "I need a pay check, so I figured I would try this out," and one time a soldier said, "I've always been really good at first person shooter games, and I can't wait to fire a real weapon at a real living target."

During this time in my new job I was dealing with another issue, a big issue. (Other than dealing with the stress of trying to adjust to life away from my child, and having to go from living in my apartment with my family into living in a small barracks room, alone, I had more serious troubles.) This other issue was a mistake, which caused me to feel quite certain the world was against me. When I first arrived to my duty station they had me take a urinalysis, and they told me that I pissed hot for drugs. Now this caught me by surprise, because I don't do drugs. And I wouldn't even know how to go about getting them, especially in a strange new place fresh out of BASIC training. For two months my leaders had me going to the ASAP program. Every Wednesday I would have to sit in there with recovering addicts and alcoholics, drinking coffee and breathing in second hand smoke while people told their inspiring stories about recovery. Every time they came around that table to me, I said nothing; I didn't have anything to say. My leaders seemed to think I was an addict, and people thought I was in denial. They felt that they were being nice to the new soldier, for my punishment could have been much more severe, so I should have been more appreciative. They were giving me a chance. Every month I had to sign a counseling form saying I had a drug related incident, but that I was receiving treatment. The leadership didn't allow me to go on leave to see my daughter, because I was still going through a recovery phase (this lasted for months.) I actually started drinking during this time, and ironically I eventually did become an addict to alcohol. I wasn't sleeping too well, I was miserably depressed, and some nights I was wishing for death...but I had to go on. I had a daughter to support, and this I was able to do regardless of my mistreatment. I ignored the thought that everyone in my unit probably thought I was a junky; hence they probably thought I was a lousy father and person. I ignored the gossip about the strange new soldier who hardly spoke, and had no friends. I didn't know where to start when it came to handling my issues, but I focused on the thought of a better future for my daughter.

During one particularly miserable day I met my first great and true leader in the Army-my mortal savior. I was sitting at my desk, after in-processing a soldier, and I was just writing my thoughts down on Microsoft Word. This older female Sergeant Major walked up to my desk and sat down to my right, where the soldiers I in-process usually sat. She just looked at me for a moment, with such sincere sadness in her dark brown eyes. Before I could ask her what she wanted, she placed her hand on top of mine and said, "Soldier, I've seen that look in your eyes before. I should have said something to him, and I'll always regret that I didn't. Please tell me what is wrong. Please tell me everything." She woke me up with her tone, and for some reason, I told her everything.

In less than a week I was called into my unit, into my new First Sergeant's office. She asked me to take a seat, and then asked me if I would like a bottle of water, or a cup of coffee. I told her I was fine. She went on to tell me that on the same day I took my first urinalysis at the unit I also went to the post hospital, (this was something I should have remembered sooner; I wasn't feeling too good that day.) She went on to remind me that at the hospital they took a blood sample and a urine sample from me also. She smiled, showing me that she was happy for me, and also sorry for what I went through. She said, "Your report at the hospital shows that you had no drugs in your system on that day. This should have been taken care of a long time ago. I don't want you ever signing on any counseling form that you had a drug related incident, and you no longer have to go to ASAP," (little did she realize I had become an alcoholic). She went on to tell me that anything on my records saying I had a drug related incident would be shredded. She apologized for everything and said that an investigation was in the works, and they were going to discover what happened. I guessed they were going to find out who in the unit swapped their urine with mine. Not long after this resolution many NCO's were transferred out of the unit, and also the Commander. I may never know the details of what happened, or who used me; the new soldier as a scapegoat.

Quite frequently, after the false charges against me were dropped, the caring Sergeant Major would stop my desk to check up on me. I knew she was the one who took the initiative to investigate into how I was handled, when I first came to Riley. And I knew she was the one who brought the issue up to my First Sergeant. Although she never admitted to this, her smile told me the answer. Before I went on leave to see my daughter, after almost a year of not being allowed to, the Sergeant Major shared some wisdom with me that I would never forget. She said, "Know the right people Specialist, and make the right friends."

I won't bore you now with too many details, although much of what I am leaving out you would probably find entertaining. My emphasis in writing this article is to inform you of where I think things need to improve in this organization, so I will save much of my story for another time.

When I was about to deploy for the first time, (a few months after returning from seeing my daughter), I wasn't happy about the news of the upcoming deployment. I wasn't horribly depressed by the news either. I knew that my job in Iraq didn't involve shooting people, (although that could happen.) My primary mission in Iraq was going to be filling out casualty reports. I felt that I would be doing a good service on my deployment, and I also knew that the extra money I would be able to send my daughter and her mother would be a great bonus.

Hypocrisy became a reoccurring theme in the Army, and I took particular notice of this on my first deployment. I made a couple of close friends when I was deployed, and today their daughter is my goddaughter. My two new friends were a male and a female, and we'll call them Casa and Chica. (Names changed). Later in the deployment these two friends of mine fell in love. They were practically pushed into each other's arms. Casa had been stressed early on in the deployment, because back home his wife (at that time) was cheating on him. Chica and I were there to comfort him and keep him distracted from his burden. Casa became like a brother to me and soon became a lover to Chica. There was another far less prudent couple in our unit, and they even shared the same trailer some nights. The female in this couple was married and the male was recently divorced. My First Sergeant was close friends with the female, and for this reason she allowed the affair to go on, (or so we assumed at the time), and none of the soldiers seemed to care. Rumors began to spread about Chica and Casa however, without good reason. They never stayed the night in each other's trailers, but they were often seen together, so people talked, and the word reached the First Sergeant and my new Commander. The FRG back home started sending e-mails to the Commander and First Sergeant asking for the leadership to have my friends Casa and Chica punished. They were pushing for them to be chaptered out of the Army with dishonorable discharge. Word got back to them through an NCO, who was talking to his wife about what he thought Casa and Chica had going on. Meanwhile this particular NCO (who started the gossip) was having an affair of his own, with a lower enlisted soldier, a private. (The FRG was a gathering of soldiers wives back home, who from what I saw did little more than spread gossip, and start scandals.) I wasn't about to watch my friends get into trouble when I knew that there were leaders getting away with their wrongs, and spouses back home doing the same.

Before this first deployment I conversed with the Sergeant Major of the 1st Cav. I spoke with him in front of my First Sergeant and other high ranking NCO's. I spoke highly of my leadership to this Sergeant Major, for I had nothing to complain about at that time. I was thankful after being allowed to see my daughter, and being set free from the false accusations against me. Oh yes, I had very nice things to say about my leadership, and with passion. The Sergeant Major left that day remembering me, and expecting the best from my leadership before our Detachment deployed. After almost a year in Iraq I wrote an even more passionate e-mail to this same Sergeant Major telling him what I had witnessed from my leadership in Iraq. I had nothing bad to say about my Commander at that time, (whom I assumed was somehow kept in the dark from what his NCO's were doing.) However I had plenty to say about the Sergeant's in my unit, and the Cav Sergeant Major considered my written words. I emphasized how my friends were being harassed and threatened. I told him how I knew and witnessed other affairs amongst the leadership. I mentioned how everyone recognized what was going on with the couple our First Sergeant favored, and how the leaders swept this particular wrong under the rug. There were many things I said to the Sergeant Major, and since these words were coming from the one soldier who spoke the most highly of his leadership prior to the deployment, he took my message to heart. He sent an e-mail to my First Sergeant and Commander, explaining how disappointed he was over the news he was receiving. He didn't mention my name. He led them to believe that he was hearing of what was going on from multiple witnesses, (which he may have, and I was just the straw that broke the camel's back.) He asked that nothing be done to Casa or Chica during our deployment, and he said decisions would be made when we returned home. Nothing happened to my friends during the rest of that deployment, and people kept their mouths shut about them for the most part. (It's good to "know the right people, and make the right friends." A Sergeant Major came through for me again.)

I felt victorious, and my friends seemed so happy over what I did. Soon word began to spread and the rumors were saying that I said something to cease the punishment that was about to befall my friends. I was glad that this particular news was spreading. I was gratified that the leaders understood I knew of what was going on behind closed doors, and even through open doors. The open doors began to close, and people were getting nervous. If anything was going on behind closed doors at this point, the actions were being kept especially discreet. I was learning to be ruthless; something the Army was teaching me I had to be.

The FRG back home were enraged when they heard nothing was going to happen to my friends, and they plotted on how they would deal with them when we returned. Well I was forming a plan also, and my two friends were going to help me play it out.

On our flight back home, there was some tension, but I was confident. Everyone was happy to be going back, and they were probably trying not to think about all that occurred before we left.

There was a Ball/gathering that was being prepared by the FRG upon our return. A planned celebration before our unit dispersed and most of us went onto other places of duty. I spoke with Casa a couple weeks before the Ball, he was stressing on what would befall him or Chica once we returned home. I reminded him of our plan, and his mind was eased.

The details of what went on before the Ball I will skim through now. (Maybe I'll share more another time if I ever write a story about these events.) In a nutshell I set up Casa's wife, only so that I could set up the FRG. I wanted justice to be served against those who were defaming the character of my friends and plotting against them. The second night, after our return to America I called Casa's cell phone, which he conveniently left in his wife's car, (before she left to go plan for the Unit Ball with the FRG.) When no one answered the call I left a text. I said some bull like, "I don't like what you are doing Casa, and your wife is a beautiful woman who has been doing so much for you while you were gone. I think you should talk to her, or maybe someone else should..." She called me after reading the text, and I sighed when she said it wasn't Casa, but his "wife." I persuaded her to meet me at a bar, where I overheard other NCO's in my unit saying they were going to celebrate their return that night. From this point, there was the quick lead to a scandal, and more gossip. There was quite a mess of information being left for the gossips, since a day earlier Chica and I signed out on pass together and everyone was talking about this incident. They were saying that Chica and I were apparently a couple now, since we went on leave together. Even Chica was telling some people on the flight back, and the day after we returned, that she and I were the ones who were a couple during the whole deployment. The only reason people were saying Casa and her were together was because he was usually hanging out with us. People were led on to believe the misinformation about Casa and Chica started with some NCO in our unit talking to his wife back home and starting a false rumor. Hence this NCO was in cahoots with the FRG back home. I wanted to redeem my friends, and I loved how confused the gossips were from my plotting. This was all just a lead up to the Unit Ball, and the grand finale to my plan.

I was seen at the local Macy's, on the day of the Ball, buying an amazing dress for Casa's wife. We ran into some of her FRG buddies/the wives there. (Casa's wife told me they were going to be there this day.) She told her friends how I felt sorry for her over how Casa was treating her, and that this is why I had offered to buy her the dress. The wives may have been confused, but they seemed supportive. Even one of the male NCO's was there with his wife, and he just kept his mouth shut and let his better half do all of the talking.

I showed up at the Ball with Chica on my arm, Casa's wife came in soon after, alone. House was one of the last soldiers to arrive, (just as planned.) He was looking wasted and depressed, and I was impressed by his acting. I danced with Chica a couple times, and then after a couple drinks Casa's wife butted in and then I danced with her. I danced with Casa's wife to a rather slow song, where I held her close. I whispered into her ear (nothing of importance); this tender action was meant for all to see and wonder, and then I kissed her cheek before the song ended.

The leaders were left confused, the wives didn't have a clue, and no one could do squat about anything. It was all so confusing, and they didn't know where to start. Many of them unknowingly offered support up to this point. At the mall when they saw me with Casa's wife they offered support, and also at the unit when they signed both Chica and I out on leave. When no one saw or bothered Casa the first days of our return, they all did their part. (Plus the fact that I knew of all the skeletons they had hidden in their closets, this probably helped too. What all did I know, or have planned?!)

Casa was left sitting at a table alone for much of the dance. Soon some male NCO's went over to where Casa was sitting to give him sympathy. They bought him another drink or two, and I believe they felt guilty for the rumors they helped spread. The wives looked at Casa's wife and saw her for what she was. In the end of the night I left the Unit Ball with Chica on my arm. Casa's wife was watching us leave, and a friend later told me, she had an angry and jealous demeanor that others took notice of at the dance.

I reiterate that my friends never got into any trouble, and they are together today and happy.

Some months went by and I became a soldier in the First Infantry Division. This unit was fresh out of Germany, and now stuck in Kansas. I was coming towards the end of my enlistment time, so I wasn't in the Big Red One for long. I learned another lesson during this time that, by the Grace of God, I was able to get through without any serious damage. The lesson was being careful what civilian females you meet at a club while near a military post. Because you just might be getting close to a deployed officer's wife, who will burn you in a moment if their husband finds them out. I was able to get out of this potential mess as well, because of knowing the right people, having the right friends. (I won't go more into that now, either.)

I had become good friends with another Sergeant Major, when I was coming close to the end of my first enlistment. I always treated this Sergeant Major with the utmost respect, and I earned his respect as well, through my hard work and constant initiative. When it came time for me to make a decision to reenlist or get out, I made the decision that I felt was best for my daughter. This Sergeant Major told me that I could get out, and that he would set me up with a job working as a civilian back in Iraq. I would be making more than twice the money I made as a deployed soldier. Or he could have me sent to the duty station of my choice if I chose to reenlist. I told him that I still needed the medical for my daughter, so I decided to stay in. I asked to be sent to Fort Lewis Washington upon my reenlistment. I made this decision so that I could get the hell out of Kansas, and so that I could be closer to my daughter who lived in northern California.

Back after I met the one of the first great leaders in the Army, (the Sergeant Major who helped clear my name during my first dark days in the Army), I met someone else also, another valuable friend. He was a soldier that was soon going to be promoted to Sergeant, a smart young man, and very business orientated. I felt that he would be a wise investment into someone worth knowing, a friend worth having. When I first arrived in Fort Lewis this soldier (now a Sergeant) was stationed there, he helped me get into the unit of my choice. I then became a soldier in the First Corps. (I had been in communication with this Sergeant before I left to Fort Lewis, and I had a leader give him a heads up, the motivation necessary to help me out.)

My time in the First Corps was from the start, a time to study those around me, to know and understand my new surroundings. Who can I trust? Who would burn me? Who could be manipulated if I ever had to be ruthless again? And who could I find dirt on if I ever needed leverage? This mindset I had, and have today, is the result of the open arms that welcomed me into the armed forces. In this new unit I decided to present myself as a very naïve, average, and shy soldier. I presented myself in this light for I learned early on when people are in the presence of someone who seems like they are of no importance; they are more likely to reveal valuable information. Sometimes leaders would speak in front of me as if I wasn't even there, for I was so quiet for the most part, but I always listened.

There were some NCO's in this unit who would go to house parties on their down time, along with lower enlisted soldiers. They would have orgies, they would drink profusely, and many times fraternization would go on between a leader and a lower enlisted soldier. I didn't really give a damn about any of this, sounded fun, and I didn't judge anyone. In my not too distant past, I had my own times of debauchery and affairs so I wasn't quick to judge. The only reason I took mental notes of all the things that I was discovering in this unit, was because I knew that someday I would need this information. If for any reason a hypocritical leader decided to make my life uncomfortable, or the lives of anyone I cared for, I would be ready for them.

This new unit came down with orders to deploy to Iraq. I had no enemies in this unit, but neither did I have anyone whom I would consider to be a friend. When the leaders called us all together into the conference room to inquire on how we felt about the upcoming deployment, I responded in a very uncharacteristic manner, (uncharacteristic from their limited perspective.)

"I know that many of the soldiers in this unit have never been deployed before," I said, "so please listen to me now and remember my words, 'leaders!' If you allow it to happen, your soldiers will run this unit while we are in Iraq. I've seen this happen before, and that is why I am saying that it would be wise to end any social relationships that you are having with your soldiers now. Do this before we deploy. And continue to remain professional at all times with those whom you work with. If you don't do this, the day will come when you realize that you have given a power to your soldiers that will be used against you. In Iraq, when we are away from our families; our children, and our spouses, tensions will rise. And the heat doesn't help. People get complacent and people get ruthless, so before we leave I think you need to clean house so that things will be better once we are there...And that way you stay in control." This was the gist of what I shared with the people in that room, my honest address to the leaders, (which I presented to them with respect. I gave them a warning.)

Interestingly enough, no leaders objected to anything I had to say, but after a moment of silence, one female private (to my right) started yelling at me. She said, "Who do you think you are?!" And "What the hell do you know!? Nothing like that is going on here now!" (I always find it interesting how people will give me fuel for my fire, without even realizing what they are doing.) The leaders watched her make a scene, while I remained silent. I just watched the reaction of those around me. Eventually she sat back down, after realizing she was not helping anything, and no one was going to back her up.

After this meeting I was invited by a couple NCO's to a military bar. (Some soldiers nearby heard the invite.) During that night the NCO's complemented me on my directness, and said things like, "You will make a great leader someday." And then they bought me a couple drinks and talked about other things not worth remembering. They clearly wanted me to believe they were nothing like the leaders I had warned them about. They were not taking notice of the fact that their socializing with me in those moments was rather contrary to my earlier warning.

Skipping through minor details, my new unit ends up in Iraq. My time in Iraq was worse this time around because I was missing my new bride, who was waiting patiently for me back home with our new baby girl. When in Iraq my leaders decided that I would make a great Admin for the Colonel, so I followed my orders and took on this new responsibility. At one point during this deployment the Sergeant Major of my new unit scheduled an interview with each of my units' soldiers. The focus of the interviews was to see what the soldiers wanted upon their return from Iraq. Where did they want to go? Did they plan on staying in the Army? And were they going to go to any leadership courses? By the end interviews she basically led the soldiers on to believe that they were going to get what they wanted upon their return. I told her that I wanted to finish my enlistment while being stationed at Fort Lewis. I told her I wanted to be in a unit that wasn't deploying in at least two years. Perhaps my requests were unrealistic, but they were also honest. She led me on to believe that this would be taken care of, and that I would receive what I asked for. If she had told me what I was asking for was unlikely, I would have simply accepted this. She gave me false hope though instead, and that was a mistake. (I'm sure she had good intentions but some things were out of her control.) I checked on my returning status with a military friend back in the states, (whose name I'm not at liberty to disclose.) I discovered that many soldiers, including myself, came down with orders to move on to different bases, or different duties less than three months after we returned from Iraq. This news was discouraging to me for a few reasons.

1.   My mother, who lived near me, was diagnosed with stage four colon cancer. I wanted to remain close to her, instead of being sent to a different duty station far from her. (I mentioned this during the interview with my new Sergeant Major.)

2.   My new wife and I had just bought a home in Washington, where I should have remained for at least three years. (This I was promised when I reenlisted.)

3.   This news, (soldiers coming down with orders while deployed), meant that the interview process was a load of false information. I was under the impression the interview was probably meant to keep the soldiers motivated during our long deployment. In a nutshell we were lied to, whether intentionally or not, this was the case. So, once again, in Iraq, I was left in a position where I had to do what I could. I wasn't out for only myself, but for the few soldiers I felt to be good people, people who didn't deserve to be misinformed, and misguided.

What left me especially upset over all of this mess was that many of the NCO's were finding ways out of the orders they came down with. In other words they found a way to take care of themselves, while not going out of their way to take care of their own soldiers. In fact, some NCO's found a way to go back home early, leaving their soldiers behind, with unresolved issues. One of these soldiers in particular, who was not helped when he needed this most, was a dreadful case. His baby girl was left home very sick and in a wheel chair. She needed physical therapy, and the wife was left to care for their daughter alone. This soldier's mother was also very sick, possibly terminally ill. This soldier was not allowed to go home early, while some of his leaders did return early, even the Platoon Sergeant, and for incomparable reasons to his own.

This time when I came into trouble, and those whom I cared for did, I had the right friend once again. This individual was not a great Sergeant Major, but a great Colonel, my Colonel. In summary, I told my (very busy) Colonel everything I witnessed, and with emphasis on the moral of the soldiers and how they view their leaders as hypocrites who don't place their soldiers needs above their own. I told him that I understood he was very busy, for he worked with the Four Star General, and other Iraqi General's. He worked with the head commander in Iraq's missions, and had greater responsibilities than most officers out there. He was under the impression his NCO's were taking good care of their soldiers, as they swore to do in front of a board of directors. He understood how all of his Sergeants had to swear in with the NCO Creed- "I know my soldiers and will always place their needs above my own. I will communicate consistently with my soldiers, and never leave them uninformed..." The Colonel had no reason to question his NCO's because no soldier had approached him with reason to, till his Admin Assistant spoke his mind.

This great leader, this great friend, the Colonel did his best to resolve the issues. The soldier who needed to go home to his sick daughter and mother was allowed to go on the first flight home. He was stabilized in Fort Lewis till his enlistment was through. And as for the other soldiers who came down with orders, including myself? Well let's just say that the Colonel was placed into a position where he had even more power over such issues, and he was determined to make things right. (This is a process that will take some time, but not too much time, and the pay off will be recognized by all involved.) Already many soldiers in this unit have been taken care of, and I look forward to this new friend and leader in my life earning his star.

As for what happens to the NCO's who may have thought they got away with something, didn't do their jobs efficiently, and only cared about themselves? Well here you go civilians and soldiers alike, please read this article again sometime and spread the news to as many as you can. I have learned in life that what goes around comes around. I've also learned that it's not most important what you know, but who you know. Even if at times you have to take the initiative to make certain that justice is served, you'll see that in your life justice will be served if you boldly stand for this. Just make sure you know the right people, and you know who and what to look out for.

Many soldiers join the military for many reasons, and as a soldier I will tell you that most of those reasons are not patriotic. But if you're going to serve your country, if you decide to be a leader in this Army, than understand you must live by the creed that you swore in by. There will be chaos, and a lack of balance in this institution, if you don't take your job seriously. If you don't place your soldier's needs above your own you will suffer the consequences more than them. If you want to be a soldier than be a good soldier, and if you want to be a leader than understand what it means to be one. One day I may be in your unit, and I'll see to it that you do understand your job as a leader. I may not be the most patriotic soldier, or the greatest leader, (and I'll always serve my family before any other person), but I do believe in the moral values that the Army Creed teaches. I thank you Army leaders for instilling these values within me, you have all helped me in some way.

NCO- "I know my soldiers and will 'always' place their needs "above my own...I will communicate consistently with my soldiers and "never" leave them "uninformed..."

The Truth Is Not That Complicated

The truth is the distractions in our nation and the excessive use of these, hinders progress, and leaves many in a kind of drunken state of mind. We're being misdirected by too much T.V, excessive partying, recent pieces of literature, (popular yet sloppily written novels), the media (being obviously bias and full of lies), the music (the sort which has no deeper meaning), the illusions (like the crazy, self obsessed life is better); these are all responsible for *tricking* us into wasting ourselves, wasting our lives. There is like a negative force, which keeps a thick fog around our heads, and blinds us from seeing what is truly meaningful. These distractions are cheap counterfeit to the true beauty life has to offer, and it's a lie if we believe these distractions can make life better.

We should be ever so thankful for the freedom in our nation, and we shouldn't take this for granted. Living in excess is the problem, (there is nothing wrong with having fun). The problem is many are paying *too much* attention to the distractions of the material world, and allowing their lives to be defined by these. Do not be tricked. Such devices will eventually take away our joy and appreciation for life. Appreciation for the finer things will decrease because the distractions hinder us from thinking for ourselves, and determining what we, as an individual, believe to be beautiful. The material worlds' distractions blind us from seeing true meaning to life. Imagination is going away because of the excessive distractions. We're losing comprehension of, and appreciation for truly genuine works of art, meaningful music, paintings of passion, novels written from the heart, dreamers who discover answers to our big problems, and bold thinkers being even bolder speakers whom believe in something greater than themselves; this is all going away because of the excess and lust for the material world. We are actually enslaving ourselves to our crutches and addictions because of the freedom we've taken for granted.

A person will spend their whole life in blindness if they believe personal offense and that which makes them uncomfortable defines what is right and wrong. People need to stop living as if they are the ruler of the world, and anyone's offense against them is punishable. Life is not that complicated, yet people, being obsessed with self destruction and being self centered, they fail to recognize obvious truths. Do not be tricked any longer by what the present material world says is important or gratifying to life. You can actually fill that growing empty space inside if you accept the truths mentioned here.

The Truths, (*which you can Google*), such as 'to believe in hope is better than to live in despair', this is something science has proven through the studies on the placebo effect, and recent treatments for depression. To forgive is better than to hold onto a grudge, for studies in psychology have proven if an individual cannot forgive then they will likely become both physically and emotionally damaged; through forgiveness somebody sick could improve their health. Do not be tricked by how your friends or the media may justify your reasons for hating a person or a group of people. (Many *so called* friends live by the motto, 'misery loves company', and this is why they purposely instigate conflicts at times. The drama entertains them and their gossip.) To love is always better than to hate, and scientific experiments have proven the importance of physical contact and affection in social and cognitive development. The biological consequences of isolation have been established according to the scientific community. These truths should be common sense, but many act as if what is right is wrong, and what is wrong is right. Many times those who strive to live in a right way or less selfish way are accused of being self righteous and *intolerant.* While those who live for self gratification, and in excess are admired and celebrated on reality T.V, and in other social circles.

An individual is always quick to defend their reasoning in why they hate someone or why they hurt those they love. People trick themselves as they come up with all kinds of excuses to why they act out in the selfish manner they do. Pathetically they feel as if when they compare their selves to someone they deem as being worse than them, this somehow justifies their actions. The individual even has the audacity to shout out, "I deserve better!" or "I have a right"! The fact of the matter is having self control, and striving to be a better person is scientifically proven to be better for the individual both physically and psychologically. Choosing to be a better spouse or parent brings hope to the next generation, while living for one's self and the material world brings about the consequences which should be so apparent to anyone who opens their eyes to this generation.

Why are we so defensive when the consequences of our wrong choices are so apparent? This isn't about taking away an individual's rights, their freedom. On the contrary this is about having self respect. The answer is about looking out for our children's rights, and providing them with a better tomorrow. If we continue to live only for ourselves, instead of focusing more on what is best for at least those closest to us, then how much more selfish will our children be once they're grown? How much farther can we fall? If you claim to be a logical person or someone who believes in science, well then choose to live a balanced life. Don't allow the distractions, the pointless trends to trick you any longer. Choose to care more about unity with others then your selfish excessive wants. Choose to forgive and be healthier. Choose to love instead of hate. Will this be easy? I expect not. But this only adds more confirmation to this is the better choice. A true sense of accomplishment is attained by overcoming the tougher obstacles in life. A sense of thankfulness comes when we realize the better life is something we earn by choosing to be a better person.

The distractions in our blessed nation are hindering our progress, but we can do our part to stop this now. Time for us to rise up! Let's choose to stop living in the haze which the distractions of the material world leave us in. Let's choose to do our part in uniting humanity so as to stand for a greater good. Let's choose to go a little out of our way today to help someone else, instead of doing something which benefits only us. Let's praise our friend or family member for their accomplishments, instead of being jealous of them. We can each choose to be an individual who will strive for a meaningful life, instead of someone who follows a blind crowd. Let us not be tricked any longer, and let's fill the empty space inside of us.

There is a feeling which wasn't there before; like a calling... The reasoning may be flawed currently or incomplete, but we're heading in the right direction... If one loses purpose in their life then they are more likely to make decisions with a cold conscience. If one can't see the importance of unity and they're narcissistic in their actions, ultimately their actions will prove to be counterproductive.

Meaning & Purpose In America

There is a problem in America today; a disease with appalling results. This generation is going through a time of war and a following recession, and many are lacking the will to overcome. Depression, Suicides, homicide, broken homes, all of these are becoming more prevalent today, so what is the answer, or the cure for our present dilemma? There is no debating that we have a problem in America today, but how did we get ourselves into a predicament that is worse than that which resulted in the Great Depression? (This may be debatable). Suicide is on the rise (American Journal of Preventive Medicine), and so is homicide (American Human Development Report; premature death by homicide is more than five times higher in the U.S. than the international average), depression is increasing (SAMHSA-Department of Health and Human Services), along with the still ever growing amount of broken homes where a father or a mother is lacking. (21 million plus children are being raised by one parent today in America, the majority according to the U.S. Census Bureau). During the Great Depression the majority of people didn't just give up and start killing each other and themselves in the prevalent manner they do today. People use to fight harder to keep their heads above the water, because they had the will, they had a purpose. And during that depression era it was unlikely that a child would be growing up in a home with a single parent, again because their parents had the will this generation lacks. Families used to stay whole even through the most struggling times, for there was nothing worth fighting harder for. These listed statistics on, depression, suicide, homicide, and single parent homes in America are not the problem but the resulting outcomes from the problem, the effects of the disease. Today many don't believe in true purpose to humanity, they believe we're an accident and that ultimately our existence has no meaning. The late Stephen Jay Gould, a famous Harvard paleontologist, doubted that if the tape of life on Earth were replayed a million times, anything like our species would evolve again. The problem is that today's understanding of the "American Dream" is not a purpose worth living for.

A vision or a will in life should never be about wealth, pleasure, or power, but this is how most Americans' view life. It is no revelation to the world that most Americans' always want the nicer car, bigger TV, more attractive partner, and a more exuberant home. They are never satisfied, always wanting more, and never really appreciating what they do have. The rich do get richer in this country and the poor do get poorer but they both have the same misunderstanding of what the American Dream was originally meant to be. The misunderstanding of true purpose to life or a vision to live by is why our nation is in the predicament that we are in today. During the Great Depression many families understood that they needed to be grateful for what they had, for as long as they had each other and could keep each other alive and hopeful, then life was worth living. Parents during the Great Depression saw their children as the future, and many of these parents struggled through life with the hope that their children would have a better tomorrow. Even through the toughest times many parents found a way to save for their children's future, and struggled to keep their family together; they understood the "will to meaning." In the least they had a dream worth living for...so they lived.

Let's look at the three main wills to life and how they are defined by three great minds, and keep in view how these ideas would apply to a family struggling during the Great Depression compared to a family struggling in America today. Let's start with Sigmund Freud who believed in the "will to pleasure." Sigmund Freud believed that the "will to pleasure" is the fundamental or motivational guide to a person's life, the will that provided purpose to an individual. "Will to pleasure," is just that, every person naturally living their lives being motivated by their own selfish desires and aspirations in life. "Will to pleasure" has nothing to do with sacrifice, like a parent sacrificing a higher position in his or her job so that they have more time with their children, or a spouse choosing to sacrifice their selfish desires by choosing to stay faithful to their partner. "Will to pleasure" would however apply to the man who chooses to abandon his family, so that he can have more freedom in life, more money, and without the burdens or responsibilities a child or wife would bring. "Will to pleasure" would also apply to the spouse who chooses to be unfaithful simply because they lust for someone else. The consequences of the unfaithful spouse may lead to a divorce and another broken home, but that's just the natural effects of a life lived in the "will of pleasure." Is there logical purpose in this philosophy? The sad truth is even today many people (who consider themselves educated and wise) believe Freuds' claim that every persons' primary motivational energy in life, (in relation to "will to pleasure"), is sexual desire. How could someone logically argue that sexual desire is the motivating factor in why a parent chooses to be in their son or daughters' life? If someone could argue this then one should conclude that this person needs to be reported to child protective services. One shouldn't argue that sex is what keeps a marriage together either or that sex the primary reason someone chooses to stay faithful to their partner. Anyone who has been married more than once can tell you that great sex isn't what keeps a marriage together. The defenders of Freud today use what some may call circular reasoning, or what L.L Brunk refers to as "trick of logic". Freuds' theories have a built-in defense mechanism, so in light of Freuds' constant readiness in relating everything to sex his defenders say "To disagree with Freud is regarded as an indication of the very resistance he predicts, confirming the evidence of Freuds' case." This is a trick of logic, it's lame, and is frequently used by religious minded people, or those committed to an ideology.

Sigmund Freud deserves credit most notably for being the first famous psychologist to think outside the box, but he is surely not the most accurate. (The troubling part is that many people believe he is the most accurate and ground breaking, and this is still being taught in many universities throughout the United States.) Freuds' methods never paved a way for people to deal with their actions effectively, but instead gave people a defense for how they behaved, giving them a lack of responsibility for their actions. This method would make sense to someone who believes "the will to pleasure", but should not make sense to a logical mind today. Trial and error has proven in history that the "will to pleasure" philosophy will ultimately destroy humanity, so it's time to evolve past this misinformation. It's worth noting that perhaps Sigmund Freuds' motivational guide in life led to his death on September 1939, when his doctor Max Schur assisted in Freuds' suicide by administering three doses of morphine resulting in his death. Freud was struggling with cancer at the time he chose to take his life and before he died he told his doctor, "My dear Schur you certainly remember our first talk. You promised me then not to forsake me when my time comes. Now it is nothing but torture and makes no sense anymore." When pleasure is no longer attainable all one can do is die, if they live in the "will to pleasure."

(Psychology departments in American universities today are scientifically orientated, and Freudian theory has been marginalized, being regarded instead as a "desiccated and dead" historical artifact, according to a recent APA study.)

Now Friedrich Nietzsche believed in the "will to power", (he was certified insane by his early fifties and died soon after.) He is most famous for two quotes, "What doesn't kill us makes us stronger," and "God is dead." Nietzsche speaks of the origins of moral values in his works "Beyond Good and Evil (1886) and "The Genealogy of Morals" (1887). In these works he says that "the theory of the perpetual elimination of the weak by the strong and the incompetent by the competent was correct." Let's think about that for a moment. Do human rights come to mind, or the poor minorities clouding up our streets during the Great Depression? They were seen as weak and burdensome by many of the wealthy, should they have just been gotten rid of? This philosopher believed that only the super-human-being or "superman"; "a superior individual who controls his/her passions and uses them in a creative way" deserved to live. "The superman's will to power would set him/her apart from the herd of inferior masses." He believed that humans' have the "will to power" in politics, culture and everywhere, since there is no God and there is no true purpose but ones "will to power".

This idea of humanities "will to power" influenced great dictators like Hitler and Mussolini; both of them were motivated by Nietzsches' writings. Living by the "will to power" has proven in history to be destructive to humanity, this should not be debatable, but of course Nietzsche would say, "There are no facts; there are only interpretations."

(For Nietzsche, there is no objective order or structure in the world except what we give it.)

Now let's analyze the "will to meaning" which renowned psychiatrist Victor Frankl speaks of. The "will to meaning" or the need for purpose in life is what we are proposing to be the motivating factor in every person's life which potentially could solve our problem. If human beings do not have a sound vision, or purpose in life, then life will lose all meaning. Living for pleasure does the average human being no good, which many realize once they reach a certain age. Interestingly enough according to the statistics at the American Journal of Preventive Medicine suicide today is highest among those of middle age or older, and those who are wealthy. Makes one wonder what these people were missing in life, for clearly they felt that they no longer had purpose in life when they chose to end their lives. And living for power is probably even more destructive than living for pleasure alone, for when one lives for power they are not only destructive to themselves but everybody else as well. This kind of selfish philosophy has proven throughout history to lead to a drop in the economy, (because profits are not being spread evenly), and could even lead to genocide, as in such cases as Saddam, Mussolini, Hitler etc. (Not going to beat the dead horse anymore.) When one chooses to live with the "will to meaning" then they can be balanced, unlike the selfish wills to pleasure and power. When you live for meaning in life you see that you cannot live alone, you need both the negative and the positive in your life, because if there was no negative then how could you ever have a sense of appreciation when coming across the positive? There could be no accomplishment in life if there were no struggles in life, and there could be no understanding of love if there was no sacrifice. The "will to meaning" is most important because this gives you a reason to why you suffer at times. Many families had to understand the "will to meaning" during the Great Depression to survive, to keep their heads above water. They understood that relationships were meaningful to life, relationships with their families was meaningful.

The families at this time were not going to give up on life simply because they were not the most successful, or the wealthiest, they lived for their families, their wives, husbands, sons and daughters. They appreciated what they had and even through their struggles they would always hope for just enough to keep those they love happy. If you understand this "will to meaning" then you will see purpose in your life through the good times and the bad, and although life seems unfair at times at least you know that there is still purpose, there is still hope. Even if a person feels that they have no one in their lives, if they stop to really examine their situation, most times they will see that there is always someone who can use a word of encouragement from them, or have them to confide in. Many times those who feel the most alone are in actuality the most selfish, because they don't realize that the people around them have their own struggles as well. And maybe if more people bothered to help one another, instead of just wallowing in self pity, then we would at least have a hope that we could rise out of this predicament our nation is in today.

The ones with power can afford to help this nation get out of debt and even war, but they are not fools. The elite can see the mentality that the average person in our nation has today, the mentality like the middle class one who wins millions in the lottery and in less than two years they are in debt; this is how many of the powerful see the average American today. Why should they waste any of their money on fools? They are wrong though, for everyone has potential to make the better decision. If the powerful don't learn the "will to meaning" then they too may eventually do what many of their kind have done before, they will take their own lives.

Victor Frankl was a neurologist and a psychiatrist who survived the holocaust. His bestselling book was titled Man's Search for meaning. This book chronicles his life as an inmate in a concentration camp and describes his psychotherapeutic method of finding meaning in all forms of existence, even the grimiest forms. Frankl was a key figure in existential therapy. Existential therapy proposes that in making our own choices we assume full responsibility for the results of our actions, and we have no one to blame but ourselves if the results are less than what we desired. His premise is that "man's search for meaning" is the primary motivation of his life. He speaks of the "will to meaning" as opposed to Freud's "will to pleasure" and Nietzsche's "will to power."

("Viktor Frankl often said that even within the narrow boundaries of the concentration camps he found only two races of men to exist: decent and non-decent ones. These were to be found in all classes, ethnicities, and groups. He once recommended that the Statue of Liberty on the East coast be complemented by a

Statue of Responsibility on the West coast, and there are plans to construct such a statue by 2010. Frankl is thought to have coined the term "Sunday Neurosis" referring to a form of depression resulting from an awareness in some people of the emptiness of their lives once the work week is over.")

The answer and the cure for our nation today is very simple, but just so that you don't feel like you are being bossed around or ordered to do something this article is presenting you with a thorough and logical explanation. This is the equivalent of a parent telling their child to look both ways before they cross the street and then the child replying with, "Why exactly do I have to do what you are telling me to do?" Since a simple answer is not enough for many in our nation today please stick with this article and the promise is that you will receive a perfectly good explanation for why you should live by the "will to meaning" philosophy.

The Army defines purpose as "what gives subordinates the reason to act in order to achieve a desired outcome." We have already gone over how when one has only pleasure or power as their desired outcome then this will ultimately lead to destruction. If humanity is to have purpose then they must have a purpose that is not destructive, if we are to survive. Helen Keller believed that purpose should be central to a good human life, she wrote that happiness comes from "fidelity to a worthy purpose," meaning being faithful to a worthy cause, or not giving up on a worthy cause. Before someone could make a giant leap into living for a worthy cause like the one Dr. King lived for they must first start with their closest family; they must serve their children and their spouse, willing to make the necessary sacrifices for their families' well being before they attempt to change the world like Gandhi, or Martin Luther King Jr. did. Truth is if more parents in our nation today would simply live for their children and spouse first, loving them and making sacrifices for them, then they would be playing a great part in redeeming our nation.

In ancient times people survived through an ice age because they stayed in tribes, where every individual did their part to serve one another, they could not afford to live for only themselves. The biggest misunderstanding today is that times are so different now, that one doesn't need to consider the welfare of others if they are to live. Granted even in ancient times there were wars among tribes, but the strongest tribes survived because they were a united people and their purpose was simply to keep their members alive. Today tribes are broken all around, even the smallest ones; the families are broken, many times because the men don't understand true purpose to life, to survival.

Religion is not the answer or the cure for our nation today, and religion did not keep the families whole during the Great Depression. An individuals' faith does hold the answer though and the cure. Faith is what the tribes, the families, and all those who have the "will to meaning" need to live and help others to live with true purpose. Religion has been the cause of many wars, and power and pleasure has been a driving force and excused throughout religious history. Granted that pleasure and power have also been the driving forces in every other corrupted organization, religious groups are most prominent in this regard. The point here is that when someone is faithful that faith can lead one into a life of meaning, and if one understands the basic concept, that unity and love is most important in ones faith, then regardless of their religious preference they can change the world for the better, and certainly contribute to the healing process that our nation needs. The main problem with religion in general is the contradicting fact that people of different religious groups (that claim to have faith in a loving God) will be hostile towards those of another religious preference for reasons that are usually more political than religious. However there are always extremists of different religions who somehow find a means of justifying their violence. There is no organization that is the answer or cure for America today, (although Buddhists seem to have the right idea before any other religion. Historically speaking Buddhism has proven to be the most peaceful of dominant religions.) The answer and the cure for our falling nation cannot be found in religion, but can be found within every individual, once they understand meaning to life, (regardless of who they call God.)

How can we live in the "will to meaning" if we don't believe there is a purpose to life? Logically we can't. Philosophically and rationally speaking only something can come from something and something cannot come from nothing. The argument against the faithful and unfaithful is the same regarding the question, "where did the first something come from?" The question applies whether you believe God created everything, or everything came from a Big Bang which came from the expansion of heat energy; where did the energy come from, or where did God come from? Suppose for a moment that just like light turns, (which Einstein theorized and was later proven,) what if time also turns, like a record. Just like planets, molecules, atoms, protons, neutrons, and even universes, what if time also rotates, or is in some way circular. What if in the end we are back at the beginning? This would only be possible if time were a circle, and since logically we know that something can only come from something else, we must conclude that time is a circle, because in this format there doesn't need to be a beginning. (Interestingly enough Nietzsche had a thought like this.) The greatest minds of our time have created a machine that cost billions of dollars to make called the Large Hadron Collider (LHC), which is the largest particle collider in the world. This machine takes up miles of space underground and the machine is expected to demonstrate the existence of the elusive Higgs boson, the last unobserved particle among those predicted by the standard model. This machine has already recreated a big bang on a smaller scale. What this invention concludes is a rather scary concept to some, but predictable to others; humanity truly can play God. Let's not assume that the Large Hadron Collider will create a big bang large enough to destroy the universe, but what if some day humanity does do this? Based on recent discoveries the thought is not all that farfetched. One of the most accepted theories on the universe is that after the big bang the universe starts expanding and eventually will stop expanding, and revert back to its source, and when the pressure is built up again the universe will explode again and start expanding like it did before, continuing this process forever over and over again. In this scenario we can see that the end is the beginning, the source of everything is also the end of everything. None of this mattered to the families suffering through the Great Depression though, right? And perhaps this idea sounds outlandish to most of you, but the point is there is reason to believe in purpose if we realize our existence makes sense.

If time is circular and we could theoretically be the cause of this spinning record then let's realize that our purpose, our "will in meaning" is all that there is. All the power and all the selfish pleasure in the world amount to nothing, only the good we do for others has a positive impact in this world. Albert Einstein said that he believed if a human being were able to use their minds full potential they would become pure energy. Pure energy is the source of all that is, and nothing can exist, function, or think without pure energy. Something comes from something, and nothing comes from nothing. Something good comes from those that live in the "will for meaning", and nothing but destruction comes from those that live in the will of pleasure or power. A child will die, or grow up mentally impaired if they don't have love and compassion throughout their infancy and toddler years, no human being can survive without relationships. Science has observed that there are opposites in everything, for even all matter has its anti-matter, and energy has both positive and negative. What will dominate your life, the positive or the negative? What kind of energy are you?

Almost anything seems possible in this world today, so no one's faith is in vain and we should all live a life of meaning. We are all worth something, and our lives do not have to amount to nothing, so we should have every reason to live with a purpose and the will to overcome. Balance is the key to survival, but negative energy does not need any of our contributions to exist, so let's focus on the positive and do what is logical by living with a purpose, with a sense of meaning to life, not simply for our fallen nation, but for humanity as a whole. A tribe/a family will stay strong and survive through the tough times and the good, because they look out for each other and they don't live with the "will to power", or "will to pleasure" mentality.

We have gotten ourselves into a predicament that is worse than that which resulted in the Great Depression because we've forgotten the importance of unity. We've forgotten the importance of relationships; the meaning of life. No family stays together because of one person, no great person ever accomplished anything without the help of others. Not even the Large Hadron Collider was created because of one person, but the gathering of many minds throughout many generations created a Big Bang. Meaning to life is most evident in relationships, so stay alive and encourage others to live, we need each other. Without meaning there is no purpose, no love, no hope, and only a disease that brings about depression, broken families, destruction, and suicide.

Afghanistan had her own wisdom to share and she was much more ruthless than Iraq…

Sep. 13th; Day of Reckoning in Kabul Afghanistan

September 13th, 2011; a soldier's account of the moments during the biggest and longest militant assault on the Afghan capital, his perspective on the longest sustained attack on Kabul since the U.S.-led invasion a decade ago, and written less than forty eight hours after the incident began…

I was reading a fictional book about the war on terrorism in Afghanistan and in the story the enemy was planning a most unexpected strike… then we were attacked. I always say *'life is either a satire or a tragedy…'*

I was sitting in the small library situated down in the basement of one of the headquarters buildings. I was lost in the story, curious to see how the enemy could pull off what they had planned; seemed unlikely. The alarm went off, "This is not a drill!" I closed my book and looked up alert. I came back to reality; not that I could have so easily forgotten I was in Kabul.

I stood up and grabbed my weapon, which was leaning against the worn black leather recliner. I wasn't nervous. I suspected there was an attempt to attack the compound which would soon be resolved like the single attempts before. I was in one of the safest posts in Kabul after all, so what was the worst that could happen?

I moved with haste out of the library, swinging doors open as I went towards the stairs, holding my weapon high even though my magazine full of ammo was still in my pocket. I was ready to follow protocol, ready to be what I am if necessary, but I wasn't expecting much. Through the next door I went at the top of the stairs and I held the door open for a couple civilians who were rushing up behind me. The alarm was sounding, and the voice on the intercom was instructing everyone to engage in putting on their armor. (I had just returned from a mission less than five minutes before I decided to go down to the library and read my book. I had transported a couple Officers to the military airport earlier that morning with the drivers training instructor and NCO. My armor along with my Kevlar helmet was still in the vehicle out in the front parking lot of the compound. I thought of heading to the Drivers NCO to obtain the keys to the up-armored vehicle, and then run out and grab my gear… The next announcement blasted over the intercom saying, "Take cover and do not exit the buildings!"

"Damn it!"

I continued down the hall and went towards the office where a couple of my Units' Soldiers worked. I was concerned somebody was going to lecture me on not having my gear. I didn't realize that this would be the least of my concerns this day.

I entered the office and gave a quick smile to my NCO before heading towards the back cubicle, hoping to be out of sight and out of mind. I took a seat and propped my legs up. I leaned my weapon against the desk and took my book out. I believed whatever was happening outside the compound would be resolved soon, so I started to read, getting lost in the fiction again.

No one gave me any shit about not having my armor or my helmet, even though the other five around me were in their proper attire. They knew I was only on this base for drivers training and they probably assumed my gear was left in the locked up vehicle. (I was only meant to be on this compound for a couple weeks of training). This was not my original station of duty...I didn't know how in that moment my own station was under attack as well, and so was the U.S Embassy near my original place of duty. If I had known this was going on I would have been much more appreciative of my present circumstances... at least for the moment, because in the next one I closed my book for the day.

There would be no time for reading, and no escape from reality this day.

The front door to our building opened, just down the small hallway outside our office. The sound of gunfire was heard, (not the most alarming sound). *Surely this was Ally fire against a single crazy bastard about to blow himself up well outside the compound?* Nope, I was wrong. This sound echoed down the hall before the door slammed shut, and was then followed by the sound of a female Soldier hollering out.

"We've been breached! The compound has been breached!"

We all heard the frantic tone of her voice, and the gunfire from outside became much more alarming in that second, along with the resonance of her footsteps as she ran down the hall and past our open office.

My book was face down on the desk in front of me and my hand resting on the back cover as I took in a deep breath. In the next moment many thoughts rushed through my mind and then seemed to become one thought; like many violent currents of water flowing through multiple streams and each leading down to one river. I was up out of my seat, I reached for the top of the solid wood cubicle and grabbed the armored vest of a Soldier who was *thankfully* on leave (lucky him). I put his vest on so fast that the motion was as fluent as taking a step. I also saw this vacationing Soldiers' helmet under the desk and put this on also. My weapon was locked and loaded in my next breath, and then I took in my immediate surroundings, trying to read those around me.

There was more gunfire, the noise being toned down now that the doors were closed. The intercom sounded off again and the announcer was telling everybody to load their weapons and stay under cover. Our Colonel came down to our office, looking far too calm considering the circumstances, but I quickly understood his demeanor. He gave orders and we followed, as his very tone and motion seemed to calm our nerves somewhat. And thankfully one of my primary concerns only a moment ago was no more; there seemed to be no cowards or fools in the office. We were all Soldiers' and nothing more in that moment, being ready this day to face the reality of what this meant. More gunfire was heard and an explosion which didn't sound too close. The Colonel had Sergeant Bee, and an Airman they called Fia up near the open office door. A female Sergeant in our office named Corona was behind them ready to cover down when it came time to switch out positions.

We were all in the office for a good hour or two, and we were positioned in different places throughout the room. The Colonel had a couple of us move anything flammable off of the desks and then throwing these into the steel trashcan, so that if any rounds were fired off there would be no flames. Also anything heavy enough to knock somebody out was moved to the floor. We switched out positions after so many minutes. Eventually I was at the office door staring down the hall with my weapon at the high ready.

I was ready to shoot to kill just like everybody else in my office. '*I wasn't ready to kill for any other reason but to ensure I get home alive along with my brothers' and sisters' near me*'. There was still gunfire being heard every so often, and when I was looking down the hall a funny thought crossed my mind. (More gunfire was heard, but it didn't sound like it was coming from inside the base). I felt sweat dripping down my nose, coming from under the helmet I was wearing, (which was too small for my head and starting to give me a killer migraine). The thought I had was of a scene in Star Wars, when the rebel Soldiers are posted in a long white hall, and they are just waiting for the enemy Storm Troopers to burst through the door at the end of the hall. Following an explosion the enemy comes rushing in, firing their weapons. Every rebel Soldier in the hall fires back at the enemy, but soon every good guy is taken out, and then you see this hallway full of dead Soldiers'. The enemy strolls down the hall after the slaughter, stepping over the good guys bodies with Darth Vader walking at the front. I wiped the sweat off of my nose and then held my weapon up higher, staring down the hall, and listening.

I heard the door at the front of the building open again followed by more shouting; a man's voice this time and he sounded angry.

"Friendly," he shouted out, making sure no trigger happy Soldiers would shoot him; the big guy with the beard upon seeing him turn the corner. (He was one of the security personnel, probably Black Ops, we all assumed). He wore a white tee shirt and a bullet proof vest over this. He was built like a body builder and held an M4 in one hand. Soon there were others like him walking around and giving instructions to Soldiers. Those of us in sight followed their orders because they just had that, '*I know what the Hell I'm doing,*' look to them, and the *"follow me if you want to live"*, look also. (At least this is the impression I had).

His heavy footprints were heard as he walked down the hall and before I saw him he shouted out again, "Friendly"! I gave him a nod when I saw him turn at the end of my hall. He just glared at me and then looked forward. He strutted down the hall as if the stale air molecules were pissing him off by being in the way of his broad shoulders. As he passed my office he shouted out a brief announcement just to keep everyone in shouting distance up to date on the situation.

"There are snipers in the building that is under construction across the street!" He said, "They are firing down at the front of our building! Stay in your positions! Where they are will be cleared soon! The U.S Embassy is under attack also and the enemy has taken over a building there!"

His voice trailed off as he turned at the other end of the hall. He flipped the light switch off once he reached the other end, and although the hall was dark the lights from the offices remained on. This action made me nervous because I knew why he turned off the hall lights; once the enemy enters the building they will need to adjust their vision to the darkness, and they will be easier for us to kill. *'Was it expected this was going to happen?'* Another bigger guy in civilian clothes with dark skin, a weapon, and a tanned bullet proof vest started walking down the hall. He laughed for some reason when he passed my office; he also stuck his tongue out and appeared to be having a grand old time. I didn't find this unnerving, on the contrary I found his confidence reassuring.

An hour or so passed, and we switched out positions a few more times. I popped a couple Advil which Sergeant Corona gave me for my lower back and head.

One of those big security guys came moving down the hall with a purpose again and he was shouting, "Give me two bodies!" Both Fia and Sergeant Bee were positioned at the office door at that moment, so they silently volunteered when they heard the need. I moved back towards the office door when they left and stood guard. I was staring down the hall again at the wall where I imagined the Storm Troopers would be breaking through.

The Colonel was still strolling back and forth in the small space in the office, speaking encouraging words to his troops and trying to ensure we remained stable minded.

Sergeant Corona asked me if I needed a break, and I told her I needed to use the restroom. She said to move and hurry. This wasn't too much of a concern since the bathroom was only the next hall over. So with all my gear on and weapon still in hand, I moved down the hall. I saw Sergeant Bee when I reached the corner and gave him a nod. I pushed open the bathroom door at the end of the next hall, situated near the front doors where both Sergeant Bee and Fia were standing guard. I placed my weapon against the tile wall and managed to avoid pissing on myself, as the sweet release was most appreciated. Maneuvering around my heavy armor, and with a helmet squeezing my head like a walnut in a steel nutcraker; these irritations were not enough to take away my gratitude in being able to empty my filled to the brim bladder.

I washed my hands in a hurry and then picked up my weapon and rushed out of the restroom. I went towards Sergeant Bee at the end of the darkened hall and asked him if he was okay. He said he was and then he took a quick drink from his bottle of water. He placed the bottle back down on the floor and then held his weapon high; aiming towards the side entrance to the building. He looked focused and steady, and I was thankful to have him by my side this day. (The Colonel had been walking down the halls on the first floor, bringing bottles of water or Gatorade to anybody who needed a drink). I moved back down to the other end of the hall in a hurry. I had just turned the corner to head back towards the hallway where my office was when a door opened and a familiar voice called out.

"I need two bodies now!" The Special Ops security guy who I saw earlier on this long day was shouting again. "I need two guards at this side of the building now!"

I heard more gunfire coming from the open doorway where this man was standing. When that door opened the light shined down the hall, as if spotlighting me, and I was the only one in the open. I saw the heads of Airmen, Navy, and Army Soldiers' pop back into their offices. Nobody volunteered. *'You really see what a person is truly made of in these circumstances.'* I had come to the realization in that moment that each of these offices were full of armed forces personnel, and most of them were cowering in there corners hoping others would protect them. (Only a few Soldiers' or Airmen were positioned down the few halls on this floor, standing guard and watching the different exits). The moment wasn't too long, as I recognized that "no body" down this hall I was standing in was rushing to fill the needed guard posts. I turned and glared at a couple faces I saw of those hiding in the offices, and then I headed on my way down the hall towards the security guy standing in the doorway. I picked up my pace, feeling my adrenalin pumping, being fueled some by the anger rising inside me. As I approached the Special Ops guard, Fia ran out from the last hall before the open door; he heard the call for two guards, and I was thankful to see him.

We didn't say a word as we rushed out through the door which was being held open for us. The security guard gave us a look and nodded with respect before instructing us. One of us was told to guard the doorway from the outside on one side of the building, while the other was told to watch his back and guard the entrance behind him. After several hours the heavy armored vest I wore was starting to bring increased pain to my lower back, and the helmet was still squeezing my skull. The Advil was not helping, but the recent change in my position was a good distraction and did help ease my mind from the physical pain. *'If this was going to go down, I didn't want to be hiding in the shadows; that's not how I wanted my loved ones to remember me.'*

We heard another explosion coming from the street just outside our compound. Later I would see on the news how a suicide bomber blew himself up there. When we heard the Apache helicopter flying overhead Fia and I exchanged a glance, we were waiting for this, and it seemed to be a long time coming. The Apache chopper opened fire onto the building in front of our compound taking aim at the enemy snipers towards the top of the under construction building.

"Hell yeah," Fia said, "Get em!"

After this incident I thought, '*perhaps things will die down now*'. Perhaps the fighting will cease for the day and the voice on the intercom will announce, '*All Clear*!' Not this day though… This day was different. Later I would hear the details on the news telling just how different this day was. The fighting did not cease, and we heard more gunfire less than an hour after the Apache took out the snipers across the street.

After a little while more Sergeant Corona came down the hall to check on both Fia and me, being concerned because I never returned to the office from the bathroom. I quickly explained to her how Fia and I volunteered to watch the entrance at this side of the building because no one else did at the moment. Sergeant Corona understood, and soon she, Sergeant Bee, and another NCO from our office-Sergeant Harris, took turns guarding this entrance; the position both Fia and I volunteered for. Our circle of Admin Soldiers' were ready to guard this important post at the front of the Headquarters Building because if not us then who?

A few more hours went by, and soon Sergeant Bee and I started handling even more duties, while Fia continued to give cover at the entrance to the building.

Sergeant Bee and I helped escort some Afghan civilians to safety, and this was a pleasant change from standing guard (where I started to not feel very useful after a couple hours).

I hadn't taken time to think of my children or my wife up to this time, not since first hearing the voice on the intercom back when I was reading my book in the library. Something inside me, perhaps instinct knew that I had to focus on the moment, each one as it passed. I couldn't afford to think of anything else but my present circumstances and the safety of those around me. On this day the moment was all there was, each one as important as the one before. The past, what I had left, my future even; none of this was as important as the moment. On this day I understood how a moment could be all one has to make the most important decision of their lives. Then came that moment where there was the calm; a moment of silence. I stepped out into the open court yard, and walked several feet out in front of the entrance to the Headquarters Building. I just felt at peace in this moment as I looked up at the darkening sky, taking off the painfully tight helmet which had been squeezing my melon for hours. I heard a sound like an explosion, but I knew this was not an explosion, but was thunder. In the next moment the rain started to pour, and I loved the feeling of the cold droplets landing on my warm forehead and scalp. I smiled as I had the thought, *'Nobody likes to fight in the rain, and explosives don't mix well with water.'* I thought of my Jennifer then, and I smiled. I was thankful to her for her love and her prayers. I realized how the reason I was able to focus on the individual moments this day was because of her and the certainty that my children were in good hands.

I went back towards the entrance to the building where I saw Sergeant Bee standing there, watching me silently.

The night was long, and according to the Intel we were still in danger of more attacks. The rain gave me hope though, and represented a cleansing process to me. The following hours were pretty uneventful, but our team remained on duty.

I started to take notice there were not so many people in the Headquarters Building during these later hours. Most people; Soldiers, civilians, Airmen, Marines, and even Special Op's were gone, being either in safe rooms, their barracks, or the basement. They must have trusted the building was in good hands, or they assumed like I did that because of the rain there was less concern now for attack.

It was quite late when we were finally relieved from our posts. I was able to head back to the barracks, remove the armor, and finally having my body relax some. I took a quick shower, and then finally went to a bed for some much needed rest.

Like I always say, *'life is either a satire or a tragedy '*. I do not know what tomorrow will bring, but the enemy is still attacking as of right now. Perhaps you even know more about what is going on in these moments then I do. Rest assure though that on one of these bases under fire in Kabul there is a handful of Personnel experts; a couple Army Soldiers', and a couple Airmen being ready to step up and do our best to get each other home alive back to you.

Reality truly is stranger than fiction… and life is comically ironic sometimes, 'this thought I have now as I look at my fictional book about the war on terrorism in Afghanistan'. At this moment I am debating on whether I have time to read another chapter or not…

The greatest responsibilities are usually never asked for…

Prophesy In Afghanistan

    The soldier was invited to a tent situated in the back of the Bazaar, where the locals were selling their products to the soldier's on base. This soldier was offered a steaming cup of tea, and then he sat down before an old man who was dressed in white garments, with skin the color of bronze.

Prophet in Afghanistan:

I asked my son to find you today. I told him to look for the name on your uniform.

Tell me what you know of the Great Harlot, who is like a parasite. I am speaking of today's Rome of course, your home.

Soldier:

(He was offended and started to grow nervous. He was holding his weapon close and he scanned the area without moving his head.)

Prophet:

I am not a fool, young warrior. You are in no danger here. I just want you to speak your mind. I know you have much to share and no one to share it with. I only want to listen.

Soldier:

I don't feel comfortable speaking with *you* about anything political...

Prophet:

Oh, don't worry young soldier I am not from this land. I am your friend. (*He smiled before saying,*) I am from Pakistan, your long time American Ally, no?

Soldier:

(The man saying he was from Pakistan struck a nerve with the soldier. He didn't hesitate a moment longer and started speaking on issues he had addressed earlier in the day with a fellow soldier.)

You say my nation is a parasite?!

Well Russia holds a large amount of U.S. bonds and treasuries.
Countries like Russia and China hold a significant part of their reserves in American securities. There should be other reserve currencies.
The euro has served as an "alternate dollar" up until Europe's sovereign debt crisis decreased its value; furthermore it's possible that the euro may be discontinued. So, if we are a parasite and they are banking on us... this makes them leaches!

Seems to me it is the same old story, our economy cannot stabilize until we recoup the jobs we have allowed to go overseas. You know the jobs young people would have normally held while going to college, like call centers and assembly line work. Maybe the US *should* go bankrupt like Russia did in the late 90's and then some other country will come bail us out like we did for them!

Prophet:

I think you're right. They are leeches, and your leaders know they are, yet they still make deals with their enemies and then pretend to be pious. America stands tall and proud and the rulers; the kings of the earth, commit adultery with her... (She is meant to be one nation under God, yet like Israel did long ago before Babylon took over; America now worships false gods above the one they claim to be under). The inhabitants of the earth grew intoxicated with the wine of her adulteries. She trades with the nations of the world, for all the nations have drunk the maddening wine of her adulteries. The kings of the earth committed adultery with her, and the merchants of the earth grew rich from her excessive luxuries. And now a voice from Heaven shouts "Come out of her, my people,' so that you will not share in her sins, so that you will not receive any of her plagues; for her sins are piled up to heaven, and Allah has remembered her crimes. "Come out of her", the angels' voice said.

Give her as much torment and grief as the glory and luxury she gave herself. In her heart she boasts, 'I sit enthroned as queen. I am not a widow; I will never mourn.' Therefore in one day her plagues will overtake her...
Then a mighty angel picked up a boulder the size of a large millstone and threw it into the sea, and said: "With such violence the great city of Babylon will be thrown down, never to be found again." Only two times in the Book is there the mention of a millstone as a metaphor. The one other time before this one was when the Nazarene said, "If anyone causes my little ones to stumble, it is better for them to tie a great millstone around their neck and jump into the sea." The distractions in America, the false American dream the middle class have of wanting to be so rich, and flaunting it; this along with the many other distractions is keeping God's children from maturing. America was once meant to be the land of the people of the book, yet she is a harlot now who gives herself to everyone, even the most corrupt King's in this world... Have you not watched the news in recent days or read about the relationship between my homeland of Pakistan and the whore? The harlot is still funding my nation, and it is my nation who funds the terrorists who kill your comrades in arms; such a circle of hypocrisy and violence. Watch how when she falls the world falls as well, because of her adulteries...

Whether you believe the verses I quoted from Revelation speak of America specifically or not, doesn't really matter, because the verses apply to her none the less. And I'm leaving out many other examples from history.

(*The prophet smiles and says*), 'Google how many people have said, "America is Rome", and the Bible says Rome is Babylon. Where is, or was the World Trade Center? Where does the United Nations gather? All roads lead to Rome, young soldier.

I have seen firsthand the way things are ran in the politics of this war; I am out here seeing it now. If there is a Babylon today, there is no doubt, America is she... And she sure as Hell is a whore.

Now I still care for and will stand for humanity in my country, in your country, and in the world. But just like the Germans in Nazi Germany should have done more to take a stand against what their country was becoming during WWII, your people need to do more also to prevent America from falling further. Are the good American's, or even the Christian American's doing more to save their country? Or are they just in denial like many of the Germans were during the reign of Hitler? Oh, and before Hitler came into power the youth in Germany grew up in the most fatherless homes in history at that time, and had the most uneducated children post war. (Germany was raped after WWI); America has no such excuse. Now proud America has beat Germany's old record when it comes to fatherless homes, and the lack of educated youths in this present generation. The scary part is your children have the education available to them, and their father's did not die in war like the German fathers' before WWII. The father's in your country just choose to not be fathers. The next generation has chosen foolishness and they glorify the fools on T.V, like the reality stars who contribute nothing of value; American's idolize them. The parents in general don't care as much as they used to, and they are still dreaming the "American dream", which has proven to be a false dream.

Hitler became the father figure in Germany back then, and he almost took over the world. Islam is the fastest growing religion in popularity now in America... Who will be this generations' father?!

Now I realize how Christianity is the most hypocritical religion in the world. I know that even before white invaders came to America and started slaughtering the original inhabitants of your land "under God," they had killed and tortured many other people in the name of Christ. I realize this all, and more. But I mention the verses from the Bible above regarding the Great Harlot, and do the comparing I did because, like any scholar, I look for truths everywhere; in all history and literature. My own personal faith is not going to be discussed here. And whether or not I believe all that I have left for you to think about here-doesn't matter. What matters is what *you* think. Does the comparison apply? And for those of you who do have utter and complete faith in the Bible, you have even more to think about now, don't you?

Soldier:

You have found more answers then I have... I look at people that pass all day and wonder; sheep without a shepherd, and wolves in many forms waiting to devour them. I agree with what you have said; Fathers and Mothers in the U.S who have left their kids to be raised by grandparents, so as to pursue pipe dreams. I hardly know of anyone that is middle class now days; most are paycheck to credit card and hopes in winning the lottery. Hard work; forget it! Everyone wants the quick rich dream...an American dream.

Prophet:

That's how I see it.

Please check out an article titled, "Meaning and Purpose in America". The focus is on the American Dream, and how the problem was not the dreaming, but the waking up.

Soldier:

Rome comparison is a real eye opener for me also. The level they reached right before their complete destruction. What a shame when history can repeat itself. I wish people would get off the antidepressants and demand back the right to live with morals. They don't have to believe in my God. But without the heart of one nation under God-what is really left? Or, without a united people believing in one cause, or in the least, believing in purpose for themselves, what hope is there?

Prophet:

 Right, right... We make the same mistakes over and over again. It's funny because one of the least liked classes in school is History. People always say things like, "Well it's boring...The past doesn't interest me. I look to the future." What the Hell?! The past is repeating itself because people are not learning from the mistakes made then. You have to understand your past to make a better future.

People have to believe in something greater than them. They have to believe they are not limited and that they can have true purpose. People live now like they exist by chance, and they have no clear purpose or direction in life because they don't believe they can be greater in a world of chance. And there is no clear purpose and direction if there is none greater than self. Those who live for only themselves add to the current mess we are speaking of.

Soldier:

I read that the next generation is, or has become the most narcissistic generation to date. If one is so consumed with their needs then they can be easily bought, sold, and deceived; for a moment of gratification. What a way to lose the heart/soul of a nation. To think *one's self* is the only one that matters; contributes to the lack of balance in this world. Christianity may be the most hypocritical of world religions, but the Sheppard whom set the character, integrity, and moral precedence never said to follow a religion. If I recall, we were to follow his example... Imagine that?!

Prophet:

 Jesus Christ is probably most misunderstood by the people who claim to represent him. I agree with all that you said and I'll quote again your words because they are so true; "The next generation has become the most narcissistic generation to date. If one is so consumed with their needs then they can be easily bought, sold, and deceived; for a moment of gratification. What a way to lose the heart/soul... of a nation".

Soldier:

Sad truth is the comparison you made is applicable. Can we avoid history repeating itself? Is there a cure for narcissism and rampant antidepressant over use? If the mind was clear and the heart cared... Can one prayer work? What would that prayer be? The end does not require anyone to roll up their sleeves and get to work on making things better.

Prophet:

 Nobody, in any belief system can rightfully judge all that Christ did, or said. This is why the atheist simply says "he was only a good man, not a God". But most amazing is how throughout history "Christianity" has used one of the most pious and peaceful individuals to express so much hate in the world at times, and they have even killed in the name of the very one who said, "Love your neighbor, and do good to those who curse you". It amazes me how humanity can turn something that was in no way evil and create world havoc.

People are stupid, plain and simple. Just look at all that is going on in the Whitehouse; all about America's debt ceiling... Even the dumber people in America had their intelligence insulted by the facade. Science has proven that the human brain is actually shrinking now; you can Google that too, kid. Did you know that Homo Sapiens Sapiens means Human Wise, Wiser? We are not Homo sapiens, Sapiens. We're Super Homo, Dumb, Dumber, and getting even dumber each generation. It depresses me, as I know it does you... How do you feel, knowing that your government is funding the enemy in my home Pakistan? And then those who rule in my land use this money to invest in the terrorists who kill your brothers and sisters in Afghanistan?! So many turn a blind eye to these truths; truths which are so evident that anyone can find them.

Empires rise and empires fall soldier. Some last long and some are strong, but in the end you can't prolong, for every empire only lasts so long. The Torah speaks on how Israel was saved by their God, but then they made the same mistakes again and fell again. They were given over to Babylon a couple times, and even became slaves to two different nations a couple times; Egypt and Babylon; America may have to go through the same thing. Who can say for certain? But what I am sure of is this; America will fall, and our world economy will eventually collapse. Money as we know it will become obsolete... Humanity will be more desperate and foolish than the young men and women before Hitler came into power... They will listen to false promises, and who could blame them?

Soldier:

An Empire can be wiped from the earth or it can grow into its next stage of life... Right? I want my children's' inheritance to count for something. I have to provide the best I can for them... But sometimes I just feel like the future is hopeless.

Prophet:

I know we'll do the best we can... I will fight the good fight from my side, and I will finish the race...You tell others, as many as you can, the truths you know. This is all you can do, and the best you can right now.

Soldier:

I will...

"When Babylon fell, the world fell! When Rome fell, the world fell as well. Now this ages Rome is falling. It's all good though, right? After all humanity survived the Dark Ages; that time of ignorance, perhaps we'll survive the next Dark Age.... Call me crazy in a couple more years, but whatever you do don't try to find me when it's too late."

"In choosing to use violent extremism as an instrument of policy, the government of Pakistan – and most especially the Pakistani Army and ISI – jeopardizes not only the prospect of our strategic partnership, but also Pakistan's opportunity to be a respected nation with legitimate regional influence. By exporting violence, they have eroded their internal security and their position in the region."

Admiral Mullen, Chairman of the Joint Chiefs of Staff

Every once in a while one is obligated to deliver substantial truths they come across; they take action simply because they must. If the masses listen then they listen, if they choose not to, well then the chance was given. The revelation of how flawed the handling of this war has been has left me severely depressed. Thousands have died because of the bad calls our superiors made...

The Origin of Our Threat & the Danger of Their Ideology

The "Word" is their most dangerous and valuable weapon, and their ideology is the largest threat to our world today.

When the "Word" is mentioned in this article we are referring to Logos: "(Greek for 'word'); *reason; refers to the internal consistency of the message--the clarity of the claim, "their" logic of its reasons, and the effectiveness of its supporting evidence."* The terrorists who attacked our nation; *they* believed in the unadulterated word of the Quran, and their interpretation of this word has been one of their most powerful weapons. Whatever message/news they spread to their people, the West, and the rest of the world they believe full heartedly to be the will of Allah.

The enemy has attacked us quite often in recent days, but thankfully no soldiers have been killed in these assaults. The victories of the enemy have been political, as they've intended for them to be. They know our media will start writing various articles about their attacks and the "word" they want to spread will do so quickly amongst their people and the world. They pay attention to people's perceptions, both here and in America. They know where to strategically strike, so that when we pull out of their country the "word" will be, "We drove them out. And now they have abandoned you. We defeated them and now we will rule over you again, never to abandon you like *they* did."

We were not properly prepared to handle an insurgency, and now the problem on our side is that there is a lack of us using true counterinsurgency methods. When we finally started to think outside the box, finally realizing it was going to take more than numbers and technology to defeat this ideology; our eventual attempts at strategy were too much *too* late. The "Word"; their Word had spread rampantly, and now the enemy believes he has succeeded in having most of the world opposing our war against the Taliban and Al Qaeda. We don't win a war like this based on how many battles we've won, we can only win by changing the enemies' mindset... We've failed though at winning the right hearts and minds... for our word has not prevailed over theirs.

Because of the choices our leaders made at the start of this war is the only reason we are in this mess we are in today. We could have won; we could have defeated the enemy fast, real fast. Hit them hard and in all the right places, strike them quickly and unexpected, which is what we did at first. The problem is that when we had them in the corner of the ring and about to fall over... we just stopped punching for some reason. Instead of delivering the knock-out punch to the appropriate opponent we went on to start another fight. When we went on to the next fight we gave the still standing opponent "time"; time to recuperate, to "think", and to build back his confidence... and time to spread their propaganda to the Afghan people. By the time we turned back to the original fighter again he was ready for us, and motivated... After watching us for years, and learning what to expect from us; he recognized our weaknesses, and took note of our patterned way of handling things. Our leaders were too arrogant and blind to realize we should finish the first fight before moving on to the next one. "In other words finish what you started, or you'll have more work on your hands later; something to remember in the future."

The enemy understands and works with insurgency, so their idea of victory is different from ours. They are so strategic minded in how they foresee the outcome that they don't care about how many battles they lose; contrarily they consider many losses to be victories which motivate their cause. The enemy is focused on winning the war, and breaking the spirit of the "*infidels*" at any cost, (in case you haven't noticed this yet). The problem on our side is apparently the lack of understanding true counterinsurgency.

Their "Word" is what drives them, and if we had struck the enemy hard and fast; knocking him out, we would have had time to present the people in Afghanistan with a better way. History has proven this method to be successful in how we handled a couple of large wars before. After World War Two- when we had hit our former enemies hard and fast; (Japan and Germany) - we helped show them a better way once the dust settled; we presented them with an idea that would prove to be promising for the rebuilding of their nations and economies. We offered aid and support after defeating our former adversaries, and we gave them freedom. Today they are two of our most trusted Allies, so we must have done something right. Now I am summarizing how we handled Germany and Japan after WWII because I'm not here to give you a detailed history lesson. The point is to remind you enough about this time in history so that you recognize when something is working, and you *see* how our handling of this present war is not the same. The enemy we are fighting today is not equivalent in their mindset to our past adversaries; they are driven by an ideology that has been withstanding for thousands of years. This war was not handled properly from the start, and in our counterattack we didn't understand the root of the *problem,* and now it seems to be too late to change their minds and show them a better way.

The ideology of the enemy is the root of the problem; what they believe the Quran teaches is the problem. (They consider their ideology to be an unadulterated interpretation.) Here is an excerpt from the teachings of Muhammad: Quran on page 117: "In the world there is only one party of God: all others are parties of Satan and rebellion. Those who believe fight in the cause of God, and those who disbelieve fight in the cause of rebellion. Then fight the allies of Satan..." There are universities today in the United States where they teach from the book titled

"Milestones", written by Sayyid Qutb; (the author being an inspiring figure to the notorious Osama Bin Ladin). This book is used today to inspire and educate those who follow the unadulterated view of Islam. Some of those who were inspired by this book are Al Qaeda, the Taliban, Haqqani Network, and others with the same ideology. The places where this ideology is being taught in the United States are widely ignored by the FBI and others who need to better educate themselves when it comes to the foundations of Islam and the teachings within the book "Milestones." (People are far too quick to stand in the defense of something they are ignorant of, just like they are always quick to judge that which they don't understand; study Islam then have an opinion on Islam, and recognize the difference between an ideology and a doctrine.)

To have had a chance at winning the war we needed to understand the enemies' mindset, we needed to understand the foundation their beliefs were built upon. Any leader who studies the history of warfare or the strategies of war would understand we *need* to "know" our enemy. Before a trained boxer gets into the ring with another fighter he studies his opponent, and he asks himself "how can I break him?" Most politicians and other government officials who rule our country do not understand the common sense I am sharing with you, and I know this because I know those who work with them. The experts say, "Politicians widely ignore us because of their financial interests with the nation of Pakistan, and they willfully ignore how the leaders in Pakistan support the main terrorist networks in the Middle East." As a Soldier this news is especially heart breaking; to realize money from our own government has indirectly financed some of the attacks which have killed our brothers and sisters in the military. And it gets worse… Through my investigations I've discovered what is hiding right under every one's noses in our nation; (which for our enemy right out in the open seems to be the best place to hide something.) The Shariah-compliant banking, sometimes called Islamic banking, is growing in popularity in the Western and Islamic worlds. But the American interest in the system, (at this time of economic crisis) is opening the door to increased Islamic influence in the American banking system. Worse yet, the banks are helping to finance international terrorism. I've discovered there are many politicians who accept Shariah Banking in the U.S today because of our desperate economy, and they realize the American Public will not believe the truth because they'll say, "How could it be right out in the open, if a percentage of the money we invest through Shariah was going to jihad? How could this be allowed?" They ignore the truth, because people these days see only what they want to see, and not what is there to be seen. None of this is conspiracy theory, and it's all there to be seen... The enemy mocks the American people as we finance their cause; they see us as complete selfish fools... for we have taken their Trojan horse right into the middle of our nation, accepting this as a gift of prosperity."

When the enemy strikes again it will be from inside our homeland, (even our President has said this). The same ideology which inspired the terrorists who attacked our nation on 911 is even more widespread today with its teachings in the United States. The ideology being spread across our nation is being widely ignored because our *great* leaders think a person's religious beliefs, or their ideology is not all that important.

In summary; we can't just ignore certain truths which make us uncomfortable any longer, and choose to just focus on ourselves alone and our personal success; this is exactly how the politicians in power today think. Our leaders who are responsible for allowing this ideology to indoctrinate and radicalize young American Muslims, they choose to look away from the source when new revolutionary activists and violent Jihadist are created. These are not conniving politicians though, they are not wicked to the core, nor do they believe they are evil in anyway. These incompetent leaders have simply avoided that which makes them uncomfortable, and they find a pathetic way to justify their actions, or lack thereof. Just like during the Civil Rights Movement when many politicians avoided having much of an opinion on the issue, and they were more concerned about what their fellow senators would think of them then what was *right*. (Yeah, they are still affected by peer pressure, just like when they were in high school.) They are no different than many of us though; whenever we see something is wrong and we choose to turn a blind eye to the problem. We keep ourselves distracted with our children or our spouse, simply enjoying our little lives in our corner of the world. All the while we avoid that which makes us uncomfortable, and we choose not to think of possible future repercussions; many of the politicians are no different. Now I am all for family values and providing the best possible life for our spouses and children, but for us to do this we can't ignore the problems in our country and the world any longer. All I ask for you to do is simple; share this news with as many people as you can. Our children need to know the truth if there is going to be hope for their future. We can't ignore the mess we're in any longer, or our children will be left with even more troubles then the last generation left us with.

The two lessons the next generation must learn:

1.   Never underestimate the teachings of your enemies; the written "Word" that those who mean to destroy you live for and would die for. Study their belief system and you'll better understand your opponent.

2.   Never overlook a spreading ideology which has proven to be destructive time and time again.

"With ISI support, Haqqani operatives planned and conducted that truck bomb attack, as well as the assault on our embassy. We also have credible evidence that they were behind the June 28th attack against the Intercontinental Hotel in Kabul and a host of other smaller but effective operations… "The Haqqani network acts as a veritable arm of Pakistan's Inter-Services Intelligence agency."

Admiral Mullen, Chairman of the Joint Chiefs of Staff.

"They can't live with us. They can't live without us…"

Pakistani Prime Minister Yousuf Raza Gilani

I would recommend you look into former CIA agent Brian Fairchild's articles and his book titled **"Centers of Jihad Support: The American Muslim Brotherhood."** For a breakdown of the problem, and the details which describe the root to the problem please check out the book listed in this article. All the information you'll need is available to you, and there are answers to any questions you may have. Be warned though; what you discover will frustrate you because it's all right under your nose, and has been for years.

Americans' must stand on the Constitution or our nation is lost...

True Democracy

True democracy should be about unity at the core, and balance. Democracy is about the people determining what is best for their nation as a whole. The people have the power and they must insure the unity and balance is not taken from them… for this could happen unexpectedly.

Perhaps democracy is only a dream *today*, or more like an illusion; a ghost of what once was. We believe in democracy, in America, because we want to. In the same manner as a faithful person wants to believe in God. The idea of a loving creator is nice to imagine, just like the idea of a political system uniting humanity and bringing an end to tyranny may also be a pleasant thought. Seeking after philosophical ways of making logical sense in how a loving God governs a world like ours; people can debate for years on such an issue. Neither side can prove though, without a shadow of a doubt that there is, or is not, a loving God. How could people prove democracy is more than a dream today, more than an illusion?

Like America, Rome was a Republic with democratic values. The Roman model of governance inspired many political thinkers, and today's modern democracies imitate the Roman and Greek models. The major difference from the Roman Republic model, (and one of the primary reasons our modern day democracy may be so flawed), is the fact our present political leaders are paid millions of dollars for being in their positions. In ancient Rome the political leaders chose to serve their nation without payment. They earned their money by other means while viewing their job as senators to be an honor, since they were able to serve those less fortunate. In the days of the Republic, before Julius Caesar shook things up, the people knew the senators cared about helping to bring a balance to Rome.

The political, cultural, and economic forces which held the Roman Empire together were removed because of Economic fragmentation, eventually leading to the Dark Ages. Following the economical mistakes made in Rome the empire continued to digress because of the **crumbling of political, military, and other social institutions, along with** *invasions* **from outside peoples, and usurpers from within the empire.** The Roman Empire held onto their particular values in politics for a time, but eventually they allowed outside influences to change these values, and wash away the foundations of the Republic. Rome started to lose their identity as others came in from foreign lands and started to change the Roman individuality. In summary, the economy collapsed, outside influences started to change Rome, and eventually too many wars, attacks, and dependence on the crumbling government brought about the ultimate fall of Rome... The loss of democratic values was subtle at first, and then by the time the people depended unequivocally upon the power of their leader, or government, their leaders had little to offer. The damage from all the mistakes made in Rome drained the economy, and helped make the populace an ignorant people who depended too much on the "*elite*" for help. Soon the Dark Ages followed after what was left of the empire crumbled...

Today, America is the great empire, or as the world believes, the great democratic nation. The march on Wall Street, the fact that more than six in ten Americans oppose the U.S. war in Afghanistan, (according to a new national poll), the protests against government spending, and our government officials being unable to unite so as to solve our present economic woes; these problems should not persist in a properly ran democracy. If the people want the issue resolved in a Democratic Nation, then the issue should be resolved, or else this is not a system of government based on the principle of majority decision making.

Instead of tyranny and a dictatorship, democracy provides opportunities for the people to control how their nation is ran. The political "leaders" should work for the people, and the people can oust them without need for violence, or any sort of revolution. Why are the people ignored today by their political leaders' in America? If the people declare, "we want to stop fighting. We want the war to end", then the soldiers' should be brought home. Despite the argument on whether something may be a good idea or a bad idea; the people determine what will be done. For better or worse, they should receive what they demand, or else face the truth that they no longer live in a truly democratic nation. If the leaders ignore what the majority want and they decide to do what *they* feel is best, (despite what the citizens want), then how can such a nation still be defined as democratic?

The idea of democracy and the importance of this political ideal can be summarized in the word "unity". Democracy is supposed to be about something bigger than one's self. Democracy is bigger than ones culture, or past, or one's personal desires. Democracy is supposed to be a balanced system where what is best for humanity as a whole is focused on instead what may be best for an individual or a group of a select privileged few. If our motive is love for something greater than ourselves, no ingratitude will hinder us from serving our fellow man. Democracy should be about love for humanity and equality. There is an idea that one's love for self is most important. Conclusively an individual will end up hurting themselves and those they love if they only depend on their selves. Every individual is flawed and their emotions lead to more trouble. Democracy *was* meant to unite a nation and preserve freedom and justice for all. It's quite clear in our nation's history that the founding fathers' wanted those in our democracy to believe in something greater than self. Sadly most live for themselves first in our nation today, and unity doesn't last… A house divided will fall.

The people believe in democracy in America, because we want to... Is this a democratic nation or a crumbling empire where the people place their allegiance in the leaders more than in the values their nation was founded upon? We are surely not united and balanced today. The political leaders cannot even unite to fix our economic crises. The people can't seem to unite and succeed in receiving what they ask for. Is democracy an illusion, a ghost of what once was? Ultimately if democracy has failed in our nation, this is because we, the people, have failed our nation.

The System Our Finding Fathers Designed

"It turns out that our founders designed a system that makes it more difficult to bring about change than I would like sometimes..."

President Obama

If one studies the foundation our nation was built upon they'll discover a reputable union meant to function for the best interest of the "people." Our government was meant to be one where the people have the power more than the leaders whom they choose. Section 2 of the United States Constitution says "The House of Representatives shall be composed of Members chosen every second Year by the People..." If positive change in America today is being hindered then are the political leaders, voted in by us to blame? Is the system designed by our founding fathers to blame?

We've had hypocritical politicians for generations, those who didn't place the people first. Every organization on this earth will have corruption, because every organization has human beings. If we see someone we voted into congress is corrupt we have a right to demand he or she is brought to court so justice could be served. The political leaders work for us, we don't work for them. At least this is how the system was meant to function. In our nation's history there have been horrible tragedies; shameful acts like slavery and the genocide of the Native American culture; the system is not to blame for these acts. Even though these embarrassing stains will remain on our nation, these horrific actions were against the spirit of the Constitution of the United States of America. Such atrocities were contrary to how the constitution defines our freedom; "to secure the blessings of liberty, which were to be enjoyed by not only the first generation, but for all who came after, "our posterity". Yes, we had leaders even back during the birth of our nation who lived in hypocrisy, and turned a blind eye to what they knew to be wrong. They had flaws, and some of them lived contrary to what our government, our system teaches. Like how some people claim a faith birthed from a pacifist loving teacher, yet they ironically murder those who don't support their faith; the system our founding fathers put into place can't be blamed for hindering positive change any more than Jesus Christ can be blamed for murders done by Christians during the Crusades. The people and the leaders may hinder progress but the foundation our government was built upon doesn't.

Because of the liberty our Constitution supports those who stood witness to the error of their ways, (multiple times in our nation's history), could not justify themselves. The Emancipation Proclamation came into being, initiated by the people who voted for a leader who recognized the hypocrisy. President Lincoln saw the need for change; the government should not be operating contrarily to the very laws she was built upon. The best way to win any debate is to use the opponents own teachings against them, and the people in our nation have won great victories by attributing this strategy. The minorities in our nation demanded change during the Human Rights Movement, and because of the system our founding fathers put into place the people had the right to demand change. Many others in our nation, those who did not suffer like the minorities; had to face the truth that in America every person has a right to the same liberties, and they have a right to demand these liberties. Article XV of the Constitution says, "The right of citizens of the United States to vote shall not be denied or abridged by the United States or by any State on account of race, color, or previous condition of servitude." The system our founding fathers created does not hinder change, corrupt humans hinder change. Even when our leaders are faulty the *people* can stand on their inalienable rights and demand a change. They can do this because our government is meant to function in such a manner that the leaders should not be able to overpower the people. If our president has a problem with the constitution of the United States of America, and the foundation our founding fathers built for us, then he has chosen the wrong occupation. We need to start teaching on the history of America again in our schools so that the next generation has more pride in their nation, and so that they may not make the same mistakes those before them have.

Our government may be corrupt today and full of people who have their own selfish agendas, but when our government was created it was the best there was, and is the best there is. We need to go back to the roots of our nation, and remember what America was supposed to be about. To blame our founding fathers is pretty pathetic. The Commander and Chief can't rightfully blame George Washington, Thomas Jefferson, James Madison, Alexander Hamilton, or any of our founders - (men far more brilliant then our leaders today) - because he's unable to fulfill his promises. Perhaps he should have studied American Government before he gave the impression he'd have the power to bring about change by himself. Let's be thankful we don't have dictators ruling over us, preventing us from positive change, and let's remember the power we have under the system our founding fathers created. The United States Congress consists of the **Senate** and the **House of Representatives. Both senators and representatives are chosen through direct election, which** is to say we the people helped create the congress we have today. The system is not to blame for his unfulfilled promises, he should have known better than to make them in recognizing how those in congress had the final say.

The only reason it is "more difficult to bring about *change"* today in America is because our political leaders on both sides can't come to an agreement on any issues, even the most important ones. They may be the worst congress our nation has ever had, but what does this say about our generation? Why do we the people allow this?

Article II Section 1 Line 8 of the Constitution of the United States of America;"Before he enter on the Execution of his Office, he shall take the following Oath or Affirmation: "I do solemnly swear (or affirm) that I will faithfully execute the Office of President of the United States, and will to the best of my Ability, preserve, protect and defend the Constitution of the United States."

Our government is supposed to be "for the people and by the people." I suppose this could be "*a system that makes it more difficult to bring about change,*" but I for one am thankful for our liberties. If the cost of freedom is the hindrance of positive change for humanity, well then we never had hope despite whatever system helps govern our nation. The President and our political leaders' should always stand in the defense of the Constitution of the United States, or in the least they better remember that we (the people) will. Because the day we don't stand for our Constitution is the day our nation falls, and there will be no *one* to blame but the people.

"Dangerously simplistic mindsets" have cost thousands of lives in the longest war our nation has ever fought...

Strategy - Know Your Enemy

What does it take to win a war against an adversary who doesn't fear death and who doesn't fight "fair"?

What could a man fear more than death? More importantly, what could the adversary fear worse than death?

Our adversary fears nothing by all appearances, for they are faithful to their cause and willing to die, or sacrifice their wives and children for the cause. The only way to truly discover what the enemy may fear is to have somebody on the inside; a spy who gets deep enough to be trusted as one of them. If you imagine that you can think as the enemy does than you would realize the only possible way you could feel fear is if you came to the realization that your cause was in vain; your faith would have to be shaken and then you will know fear.

Why must we depend more on strategy than force of numbers against our enemy? The answer to this should be obvious but here is the elaboration; one enemy kills more of us with one IED than we kill them with an entire squad firing weapons. We must recognize how the enemy fights and find our own experts in guerrilla warfare who can fight fire with fire. When a convoy travels, have an aircraft following from above, gaining a bird's eye view on what is going on down below and seeing what lies ahead of the Ally convoy. The first couple vehicles should be up armored, preferably strikers, and the middle vehicles should also be up armored or strikers. After an IED goes off, (if it's not spotted ahead of time), have communication coming from above telling those in the convoy down below where the enemy has been spotted, (if possible). In every convoy have there be IED experts travelling along with a squad of Rangers.

This is for protection and support of the other soldiers' in the convoy. Once the enemy sees this system working for us they will start to become discouraged over the lack of kills they accumulate. All of their thought and hard work bringing in little value will force them to change their strategy. (Even if my suggested method above seems an unlikely prospect, the fact of the matter is we have to do something different than we have been doing). To do the same thing over and over again, while seeing that we suffer the same results every time is the sign of insanity, so let's not do this. In summary, let's not be insane, let's recognize the enemies' style, and let's adapt.

Why must we break their spirit and take their pride?

All they have is their pride, and faith in their cause, and once we take these from the enemy he has nothing. The question is; are we willing to do this and risk flouting our hypocritical good guy image? If we are not willing to break the enemies' spirit, so as to take their pride and the faith in their cause, then we cannot win.

And what of our own soldiers, you may wonder. What has the enemy discovered when it comes to defeating our brave warriors? Well they know our fears, our predictable routines, and they surely know how to tear down our moral and break our spirit. Why does the enemy know these things? They see how our media shares everything and for the most part doesn't support our cause in fighting this war. The enemy sees how easily manipulated the American public is. They see how the average American civilian's number one fear is "what do other people think about me?" Or, "am I accepted by my peers?" This tells the enemy that our next generation of leaders is going to be weaker than those before, and they say "thus their resolve will be easier to dissuade." And they also see how easy information is to come by in our country. (We are thankful for our freedom, but the truth is the truth, and will not be sugar-coated in this article.)

Our own soldiers will fight for our freedom even in the face of death. But they do have primary fears; they fear losing their families, and losing purpose in their lives. They grow weary in having to leave their spouses and children every other year, and seeing no end to the waging war in sight. They grow frustrated when they see little positive change within the land where they fight.

Our warriors learn the routine, and they see their leaders making the same mistakes over and over again. They grow frustrated when they see many of their undeserving peers becoming the next generation of leaders. They take notice on how one does not gain promotion in the Army because of the hard work they do, or how good of a job they do. Nor does a soldier earn a raise when they are placed into a position which should be worked by somebody higher ranking, even if they handle the responsibilities inherent in that position. When many of our next generation of leaders proves to be unable to provide purpose, direction, and the motivation necessary to accomplish the mission the moral of our young warriors decreases. When they see complacency at times and the mistakes being made by their superiors, their moral weakens.

The suicide rate is increasing rapidly in the United States Army; each year since we have been at war in Afghanistan the numbers have raised. Our Leaders' are trying to figure out why this is the case...The enemy is proving to be successful at breaking our spirit and taking our pride, one might assume.

What does it take to win a war against an adversary who doesn't fear death and who doesn't fight "fair"? KNOW YOUR ENEMY!

Deep Thoughts In Afghanistan

Thoughts I have while looking at all the insanity around me, as we pretend we have a clear purpose worth fighting for out here. These thoughts are quite random, but that's just the point; to show you the random thoughts a young soldier has while in these unique circumstances.

The Army definition of Leadership is being able to influence your soldiers' by providing them with purpose, direction, and the motivation necessary to accomplish the mission and improve the organization. Up till the day of deploying my unit had not been provided with a mission; we had no idea what we would be doing once we arrived in theater, hence we had no clear purpose, direction, and certainly no motivation. One wonders in this situation w*here should we even begin when it comes to improving this organization?* Are these circumstances tragic, or simply satirical?

The Marine was the driver, a lean and fit individual who moved with the utmost ease as if he wore only a cotton tee instead of a heavy Kevlar plated vest. He jumped up onto the driver's seat, looking quite entertained over the fact that the new soldier, *that's me*, was greener than Leprechaun piss.

"You ready," he asked, looking back at me. "Not afraid are you?"

I nodded and gave him a thumbs up. I was as ready as I could get for somebody who had never been on a convoy through Afghanistan. I certainly never would have imagined I'd be riding through the city of Kabul in a single vehicle, with no other for cover from behind or ahead. This was my first day on the job in Kabul, and I was about to leave a base which I am not at liberty to mention the name of here. On this day all I knew of my job was that it would involve driving outside the wire once a week to pick up awards from another base, in the safety of an up armored SUV, with a Marine Corporal as the driver, and an Air Force Sergeant in the front passenger seat. All of us were personnel soldiers', this means we primarily worked in an office environment for the most part. My thumbs up, along with the large smile I gave the Marine was my silent way of saying, *I'm ready to do something crazy.*

As soon as we left the base and began driving through the chaotic streets of Kabul, (where nobody knew how to drive), the following random thoughts crossed my crazy mind;

"When you're thankful for something positive in your life understand that you would have nothing to be thankful for if there was no negative."

"Why do people think that when they swear on some ones grave this action counts for something? Swearing on a dead person shouldn't count for anything... they're dead! Are they going to vouch for your integrity?"

"Am I the only one who thinks the expression, "I give you my heart," sounds really morbid? Not to mention highly unlikely."

"The next time somebody who doesn't really know me walks up to me and asks, "Have you ever had one of those days?" I'm going to reply with "which day is that?" followed by "I ate a baby this morning and now I am miserably constipated and suffering with heartburn. Is this the kind of day you're asking me about? Because in that case-yes. Yes, I have had "one of those days."

"I believe I'm crazy... because in my crazy reality all technology runs on dead dinosaurs which have transformed into black ooze that our world leaders fight over. You see in my crazy reality our world desperately needs the dead dinosaur ooze to save our economy. And on that note I know I'm crazy because everybody spends imaginary money which brings the entire world economy into debt, and the leaders in my country talk about needing to raise the imaginary "ceiling of debt" to save us from our loss. In my crazy world in my crazy mind this dead dinosaur ooze which the world economy needs to save us from the accumulated debt brought on by our spending of imaginary money is also

destroying my crazy world with toxic fumes...Somebody help me, because I'm crazy!"

"I think it's funny how we as human beings can destroy each other and progressively all of the life on the planet and when a natural disaster like a tsunami or an earthquake kills thousands we say "What a cruel world!" Or "Why God!?""

"I think it's funny when somebody says, "I didn't deserve this!" following a break up, or a divorce. What do they even mean? If you were such a good spouse then why not have peace of mind knowing that your former partner has recognized how it's they who don't deserve you."

"The next time somebody I work with asks me "have you ever done something you really regret," I'm going to reply with "have you ever listened to yourself?""

"One time I heard somebody say "Everything is meaningless!" To which I felt like saying "I don't understand what you mean...""

"You know the one thing that makes me angrier than dealing with a lazy, procrastinating person; stubbing my toe on the doorframe while on my way towards the bathroom, because I'm desperately needing to take a piss in the middle of the night."

"Why is it that whenever somebody loses their home, job, or a loved one everybody has to ask them "Are you all right?" People are sick!"

"I have discovered that I frequently enjoy the use of metaphors. Someday I hope to foster a child and I will name the kid resentment. Or is the expression "harboring resentment" instead of fostering? In that case never mind."

"You know what makes me want to laugh while working in an office environment; when somebody runs into my office and tells me that they are "in dire *need of some assistance." In less they just accidentally punctured an artery with their pen, or somebody in the cubicle next to them just offed themselves because they finally had too much of the mundane routine; they're not in dire need."*

"I love it when somebody passionately makes a promise which they can in no way keep like, "Everything is going to be all right!" No, everything is not going to be all right. You just lied to my face. I am certain that there is allot in this world that is pretty freaking far from "all right." For starters I know that you're a liar."

"People say "life is a bitch and then you die". That is not true! I tell you that life is full of promise and hope...and then you die. In less you have Jesus of course...but even then in one way or another you're still going to die."

*"The older generation of machismo men ask "Where are all the **men** at!?" What do they mean? There are all kinds of men around these days. The problem is they are all asking the same question; "Where are all the men at!?"*

"People ask, "Whatever happened to the American Dream?!" I say-nothing! The problem is the waking up! Too many people have been dreaming for so long and now they all have to wake up to reality."

"I love how it has been said one should respect the wisdom of their elders. If my elders are so wise than how come my generation has been left with two wars where the enemies were made by my elders, an economy that has gone to shit, and no social security for when the time comes for my old ass to relax and claim to be wise?"

"One should always strive to provide purpose and direction to their lives, and they should seek after the motivation necessary to press onward towards a clear objective in life."

"If you cannot govern your own life and discover your own purpose then how could you possibly provide purpose to someone else?"

"If you lack the motivation than how can you motivate others?"

"If you have no clear mission to lead, through which you can also improve the organization where you work, then you are doing nothing."

"I would have never known there were so many aspiring poets in the military if not for the use of public bathroom stalls in Afghanistan. I'm glad they don't quit their day jobs."

"The distractions in our day to day lives back home keep us blind to the reality around us, and ironically reality shows add to this problem."

When our vehicle made it through the city in one piece and then passed through the gates onto the next base I had some revelations;

"Life is either a satire or a tragedy, there is no in between. It all depends on how dark your sense of humor is."

"You can either laugh at how ridiculous everything is in this world, or cry."

Once we drove through a second gate the Marine looked back at me and so did the Airman. I was laughing hysterically, and the looks on their faces made me laugh all the harder.

The research continues; the search for the seeds which spawned the largest problems with mankind... I ask, 'why?' Then I look for the answers… and I find them.

Problem With Man - Decreasing Testosterone Because of Micro Evolution

Before the increase in technology, there was a simple system that seemed to work.

The irony is that along with our growth in knowledge, when it comes to technology, we have become far more foolish when it comes to the dispensation of humanities survival. Long ago, Man was the hunter and provider of food, having to be strong to defeat a mighty mammoth, or to defend his tribe (women and children) against invaders and wild animals. Mans' testosterone levels had to be high, for he was relied upon more for his strength and agility then for his technical skills.

The Woman was the nurturer, the one who cared for the children, keeping them fed, warm, and fit. Her estrogen level had to be higher for the care she provided for her family. She kept the camp or cave comfortable for the children and the Man who was the bringer of the food and protector of her and her children. Women would also gather fruit and vegetables to provide more nutrients than just the protein of the kill the Man would bring home. Women nurtured the children, who would grow up in a world where they would endure so much, while men killed and fought for the survival of the tribe. Man and Woman relied upon each other and brought a kind of balance to their children who also grew up to follow the same system. This is the way it potentially worked for the most part in the days before technology. Today things have changed, and there is a problem because of this change. The problem is that there is a decrease in Men (necessary providers), hence a decrease in testosterone, hence a severe loss of balance. An estimated 24.7 million children (36.3%) live absent their biological father. --Source: National Fatherhood Initiative, Father Facts, (3rd Edition): 5.

According to 72.2 % of the U.S. population, fatherlessness is the most significant family or social problem facing America. --Source: National Center for Fathering, Fathering in America Poll, January, 1999. The decrease in Father figures is worse in recent years than it was after WW1, where the lack of fathers in Germany resulted in the young men following Adolf Hitler, and being more susceptible to his promises and apparent care for them as they saw him as a father figure.

These recent generations of young men who grow up without a Father have also joined the ranks of men who have abandoned their children, or men who don't know how to properly be there for their children even when they are in their lives.

The increase in single mothers has brought about the change in evolution (micro evolution), which we have been recently experiencing. (Microevolution is the occurrence of small-scale changes in allele frequencies in a population, over a few generations, also known as change at or below the species level.)

These changes may be due to several processes: mutation, "natural selection", gene flow, genetic drift and nonrandom mating.) Since there are fewer men (apparently) needing to be Fathers/Providers for their tribes, the women have taken over both roles, as provider and nurturer. So as the rule of micro evolution teaches us, humanity has had to adapt and the result (because of what nature sees as a major change) is the decrease of testosterone, and the decrease of Men. Nature sees that men are no longer as necessary as they were in the past, for the Woman has had to evolve and be Man instead. My obvious theory is that the continuing decrease of fathers/real men (necessary providers) has resulted in the evolutionary change, which is the steady decrease of testosterone in men.

In men testosterone builds muscle, enhances sex drive, elevates the mood, prevents osteoporosis and increases energy. Men's testosterone levels have been decreasing since the 1980's. Apparently, the levels dropped by one percent each year from 1987 to 2002.The researchers postulate that a decrease in testosterone levels may be caused by obesity or cigarette smoking. Note (The increase in victims of ovarian cancer may be because of the increase of testosterone in women.) Testosterone is the primary male sex hormone and plays an important role in maintaining bone and muscle mass. Low testosterone levels have been linked to health problems, including lowered libido and diabetes. Over the past two decades, levels of the sex hormone in U.S. men have been falling steadily, a new study finds. According to the FDA (food and drug administration), more than four million men experience low testosterone levels. Around 95% of them fail to seek any treatment, often because they just take the sign as a normal part of getting older.

So because nature sees that Man is no longer needed to provide for the women and children, and Man chooses not to provide when he could, the whole world will have to change, or "evolve". Testosterone will continue to decrease, men will become weaker with each passing generation, and women will become stronger.

The reason we have become far more foolish when it comes to the dispensation of humanities survival is because the majority of men do not want to be men anymore. Many have become lazy, depending on technology to survive, caring only about himself or his mommy, (who was both the nurturer and provider for him). On an average the male sex does not know how to be a man, does not know how to provide for or protect the women and children, so nature has decided that they are not as necessary.

Our present way of doing things, our present system is not working, so I suppose the best that we can do is start with ourselves and our own families.

Here are some facts about the negative effects of a lack of men/fathers: Children who were part of the "post war generation" could expect to grow up with two biological parents who were married to each other. Eighty percent did. Today, only about 50% of children will spend their entire childhood in an intact family. --Source: David Poponoe, American Family Decline, 1960-1990: A Review and Appraisal Journal of Marriage and Family 55 (August 1993).

With the increasing number of premarital births and a continuing high divorce rate, the proportion of children living with just one parent rose from 9 percent in 1960 to 28 percent in 1996. Currently, 57.7 percent of all black children, 31.8 percent of all Hispanic children, and 20.9 percent of all white children are living in single-parent homes. --Source: Saluter, Arlen F. Marital Status and Living Arrangements: March 1994., US Bureau of the Census, Current Population Report. p28-484. Washington, DC: GPO, 1996. US Bureau of the Census. Statistical Abstract of the United States 1997, Washington, DC: GPO, 1997.

The U.S. Department of Health and Human Services states, "Fatherless children are at a dramatically greater risk of drug and alcohol abuse" --Source: U.S. Department of Health and Human Services. National Center for Health

Statistics. Survey on Child Health. Washington, DC, 1993.

Children who live apart from their fathers are 4.3 times more likely to smoke cigarettes as teenagers than children growing up with their fathers in the home. --Source: Stanton, Warren R., Tian P.S. Oci and Phil A. Silva. "Sociodemographic characteristics of Adolescent Smokers." The International Journal of the Addictions 7 (1994): 913-925.

Children in single-parent families are two to three times as likely as children in two-parent families to have emotional and behavioral problems. --Source: U.S. Department of Health and Human Services. National Center for Health Statistics."National Health Interview Survey." Hyattsville, MD, 1988.

Three out of four teenage suicides occur in households where a parent has been absent. --Source: Elshtain, Jean Bethke."Family Matters: The Plight of America's Children." The Christian Century (July 1993): 14-21.

In studies involving over 25,000 children using nationally representative data sets, children who lived with only one parent had lower grade point averages, lower college aspirations, poor attendance records, and higher drop out rates than students who lived with both parents. --Source: McLanahan, Sara and Gary Sandefur. Growing up with a Single Parent: What Hurts, What Helps. Cambridge: Harvard University Press, 1994.

Fatherless children are twice as likely to drop out of school. --Source: U.S. Department of Health and Human Services. National Center for Health Statistics. Survey on Child Health. Washington, DC; GPO, 1993.

School children from divorced families are absent more, and more anxious, hostile, and withdrawn, and are less popular with their peers than those from intact families. --Source: One-Parent Families and Their Children: The School's Most Significant Minority. The Consortium for the Study of School Needs of Children from One-Parent Families. National Association of elementary School Principals and the Institute for Development of Educational Activities, a division of the Charles f. Kettering Foundation. Arlington, VA 1980.

Children in single parent families are more likely to be in trouble with the law than their peers who grow up with two parents. --Source: U.S. Department of Health and Human Services. National Center for Health Statistics. National Health Interview Survey. Hyattsville, MD, 1988.

Adolescent females between the ages of 15 and 19 years reared in homes without fathers are significantly more likely to engage in premarital sex than adolescent females reared in homes with both a mother and a father. --Source: Billy, John O. G., Karin L. Brewster and William R. Grady. "Contextual Effects on the Sexual Behavior of Adolescent Women." Journal of Marriage and Family 56(1994): 381-404.

Americans unresolved father problems.
Over half of Americans agree that most people have unresolved problems with their fathers. Cumulatively, 55.6% agreed with this statement, up from 54.1% in our 1996 poll. More non-whites (70.4%) than whites (56.3%) were in agreement. Interestingly, the generation who has experienced more father absence, 18- to 24-year-olds, displayed the highest level of agreement (67.2%). Income was also a differentiating factor: of the respondents making $25,000 or less, 70.1% agreed, compared to only 48.0% among those who make more than $50,000. Source National Center for Fathering 1996.

The recognition of the present day problems and the fear over how blind many leaders seem to be is increasingly depressing... If our founding fathers saw us today they would weep.

Alliances With Other Nations No Longer A Gray Area

People have heard the expression "being in the gray area". Do we know what this means anymore when it comes to our alliances with other nations?

George Washington would turn over in his grave if he were to see the nations we call allies these days. He warned against having a long term alliance and funding outside nations, and he warned about the potential corruption in our nation caused by such alliances. Today we send more money to those who should be considered enemies then we do those who treat us like an ally should.

Afghanistan wants more money from us when it comes to helping them rebuild their nation, and our Commander and Chief wants to provide these funds... What is the point? When President Karzai and the Afghan government thinks setting a woman free from ten years of prison, where she was placed for being a victim of rape, just so that they could force her to marry the relative who raped her; why should we support such a government financially? Where is the justice in this? What is the point to sending billions of dollars worth of support for Afghanistan when we can't do more to help the poor women and children in their nation. We look past this nation's corruption and act as if we believe our weapons and money can fix their nation... Are our leaders' complete fools? If we allow this twisted sense of justice in their nation; this corruption, then there is no amount of money that can help them. To fix a problem one must go to the root of the problem. We need to cease the funding towards such corrupt nations, for this is not being in the gray area, this is being in the shadow; for we are inhibiting their progress by allowing their injustice, and then paying them while doing this. We should use this money to help our own nation instead, where we have more of a hope in taking care of our women and children.

Allowing freedom of religion in our nation is a grand gift bestowed to us. But when we fail to recognize the difference between a dangerous ideology and a religion we hurt our people and our nation. Just like we wouldn't allow a Christian cult where children are married to adults, or allow Pastors' to have several wives who are under age, neither should we allow an Islamic ideology that teaches true Islam is one where one condones the killing of an Infidel; any non-believer. Yet as crazy as it may sound one of the fasted spreading ideologies of Islam in our nation is one inspired by the book titled "Milestones". This book was the number one inspiration for the leaders of the Taliban, Al Qaida, and the Haqani Network... And we have the audacity to wonder where our recent homegrown terrorists came from.

When did we start believing that providing support or freedom to those who wish the American people harm is being in the gray area? This is wrong, period. How is this misunderstood?

Being tolerable of one's rights, does not mean we should ignore the obvious threats. In Afghanistan they will arrest a woman for being raped, and she may even be killed before this can happen. Supporting a government who allows this, and calls this justice is just as bad as allowing the same injustice in our own nation.

Doing the right thing is usually not easy, and people may suffer, but this doesn't mean we have a right to look the other way when the wrong thing is happening... This makes us cowards and no better than the perpetrators of the crime we choose to ignore. Contrarily after the crime has taken place right in front of us our leaders shake the perpetrators hand and then give them money and support.

We are no longer justified when it comes to our alliances with those who contradict and despise our nation's liberty. We are no longer in a gray area, but instead we've become an accomplice to their injustices.

Does faith have any value, or do only fools believe in some sort of meaning to life?

Trick of Logic

What kind of fellowship can light have with darkness?

The most asked question directed towards religious leaders is not, "Can you prove there is a God?" The question asked even more is, "If God is Love, then why does he allow so much evil?"

The philosopher Epicurus thought he was making a good point when he said, "Either God wants to abolish evil and cannot; or he can, but does not want to. If he wants to, but cannot he is impotent. If he can but does not want to, he is wicked."

Epicurus sounds pretty clever, huh? I know he thought everyone would be pretty impressed with his statement, which I was ten years ago. I call it a "trick of logic" statement, and I'm going to do the same trick he just did, then I'm going to explain to you exactly what we did to mess with your head.

"Either everything came from nothing, and nothing is the source of everything; or everything can't come from nothing, because everything would amount to nothing. If everything is meaningful then it came from something. If everything has meaning then there can't be a logical concept of nothing."

This trick has been done many times in many debates throughout history. It's an easy trick to do, because humanity has a sense of logic that cannot be denied. It's easy to brainwash someone using statements like mine, or Epicurus, because we give the impression that if you believe in one thing then you are a fool, because that one thing you believe in clearly contradicts something else, and that something else is always the exact "opposite" of what we are trying to disprove. This kind of trick reminds me of a quote from a character in the movie Men in Black; "A person is not stupid, people are stupid." A single person can easily brainwash a multitude of people, but that multitude cannot so easily brainwash others into joining their cult, however an individual may be able to, if he or she, is an adequate and convincing enough speaker. You notice how there is a full circle much of the time? This is what happens when someone uses a trick of logic statement, they in some way go back to where they started.

It's not so easy to do this trick if you're starting with such statements as "There is no God," in less the atheist goes back to the "problem with evil," like Epicurus did, and rephrases the statement to something like, "God cannot be, because humanity defines him as Love, so therefore if God is then we should not have a concept of evil." Or something more simple like, "There cannot be a loving God because we have so much suffering in the world."

Before we see the answer to the big question, the question which an atheist always uses to stump the faithful, allow me to state the obvious; something comes from something, and everyone knows that logically when we examine something that is complex we must conclude that it came from an intelligent source. And regardless of how many billions of years (one may assume) went by before the creation of the living Cell, for example, we all should know that it's one hell of a roll of the dice for something that complex to come into being by chance. For example, imagine a car (which is far less complex than a cell), is left in pieces spread throughout a junk yard; we all know it's pretty unlikely that that car is going to someday put itself together by random chance, even if left in pieces for millions of years. And even if the car somehow does come together because of wind and other natural sources of luck over the course of many years, who is going to start the vehicle? So again I reiterate the fact that if we are trying to do the trick of logic statement from an atheist perspective it only works if we judge the existence of God by assuming because we have impiety/evil in the world there can be no "just" God, like Epicurus sought to prove in his statement.

Before there was the technology to study the air we breathe, how could we prove to someone that we were breathing air? No one would ask you such a question like "Are you breathing air," because they know the answer as well as you, "Yes, I am breathing, so therefore I am breathing air." But let's assume they did ask you that question, and when you gave them your answer they shot back at you with another question, "How do you know you're breathing air? Can you see it?" You probably wouldn't really know how to reply. I mean what could you say?

"I just know, because I can breathe." I know this is all stoner talk, trying to look too deep into issues that in reality are not that complex, but this is what you have to do if you don't want to believe in an intelligent designer/God.

What atheists like to always come around to as a valid point is, "Just because we can't disprove the existence of God, doesn't mean that you can ever prove there is God." After seeing all that I have, and studying evolution, biochemistry, microbiology, history, philosophy, and so much more, I say if that is a valid point, then it's the same as saying, "Just because I can't disprove the existence of air, doesn't mean that what you call air is truly air at all. Because I can't see it, and neither can you."

The mathematical structure of DNA is not called the "blue print" of life by accident; it's called the blue print of life, because that's what it is; a design plan mapped out, showing the detailed structure of life. The living Cell is not called "complex", because it's a little complicated, it's called complex because it's far more complex than anything Man has ever "created." The eye did not, in Darwin 's own words, "give one chills," because it was a simple structure, it gave Darwin chills because he could not come up with an evolutionary explanation for something that was as essential as the eye. When an atheist examines all of these wonders with our new knowledge in microbiology they tell the ignorant public that they see no need for a God, and the ignorant public shrugs their shoulders and says, "People smarter than me say they see no evidence of God, so who am I to argue? They know more than I do, and I don't even "care" to understand. Besides it's boring, and I would rather do something else. I already know there is no God, because I can't see him."

Alright, I'm not going to go through the details to prove to you that there is a God, not on this essay. But before I answer the really big question, I'm going to quote an excerpt from a discussion between the theologian Ravi Zecharia and a college student (whose name is not important enough to remember,) then I'm going to tell you how many scientists perceive God, and then we'll get to the answer.

"Meaningless!" The student stands up and shouts in anger, "Everything is meaningless!"

"You don't believe that," Ravi says calmly before yawning.

"Yes, I do!" The student exclaims loudly. "Everything is meaningless."

"You are saying that, but you don't *mean* that, now, do you?"

"Yes I do!"

"If what you just said is true," Ravi says as he takes off his glasses and begins wiping the lens on his coat, "Then what you have just said could not be meaningful. You can sit down now, because you have nothing to say."

The student sat down at a loss for words...

Ok, now, we know that something comes from something. So who made God then? Good question, huh? Where did God come from? Well the atheist has the same problem when it comes to energy. Actually it's not really a problem at all, because all scientists have no problem accepting the fact that energy is the source of all that is, and without energy there could be nothing. Energy is the only substance that always has been and always will be, having no beginning and no end, kind of like alpha and omega. (We're not going to go into the whole, how do we know there is energy if we can't see it bit.) An atheist may have their faith in energy as the source of all life, giving it no personality, or imagined form, while the faithful call "it" God.

Now the big answer to the big question; (I am assuming this is being addressed to recently converted agnostics now), "If God is Love, then why does he allow so much evil?" Well here are the facts; If God is Love, as more then a few religions say, then logically he cannot be Hate. If God is Just, he cannot be unjust. If he is the Light (this is important now), then he cannot be the Darkness. The answer is there, and it is similar to the whole Ying and Yang idea. It's all the ideas mixed together though.

You see everyone believes in freedom, and everyone wants more of it, even when it's all there for you. Even if humans make laws, you are free to break them if you're clever enough to get away with it, or rich enough. But everyone wants peace on earth as well as freedom, and because people want peace they make laws. So People want perfection, yet they want freedom, but therein lies the paradox. How can one be free without opposites to choose between? And if all was perfect, (a preposterous assumption), then there would be no opposites to choose between, because opposites are defined by extremes. Right and wrong, light and dark, a truth or a lie, love or hate, or to forgive or hold a grudge, to accept, or deny; these are the choices that define true freedom. With there being no choice there would be no sense of appreciation, accomplishment, or peace of mind. Don't you see the idea of perfection is most imperfect? Because all that is negative defines all that is good.

From a logical perspective, I think the Christians as well as the other major religions have it wrong. Because they say in the beginning there was God, and there was nothing else. There was no beginning before the Big Bang, because there was not time. Or perhaps they indirectly separate God into two halves, and theoretically science can separate energy into two halves. There is positive energy, and negative energy, and obviously they are opposites, but these absolutes always have been and always will be, because they define each other. I call them quite simply the Light and the Darkness. So if when the religious groups say in the beginning there was only God, and they believe that like energy, God can be separated into two opposite halves then maybe I can agree that in the beginning there was one God.

The positive energy, or the Light, did not create all that is evil, for the Light is supposed to be the source of hope, being what shines through the darkness. The negative energy/ the Darkness is the source of evil; pain, fear, death, and everything that can lead to death, or everything that brings pain to others and the world. Whichever source humanity decides to invest in, or feed the most, will be the force that takes over more. Since we can see both Light and Darkness as two different kinds of energy, then let's look at it from that perspective and realize that for every action there is a reaction, for every negative there is a positive. Don't blame the Light for what comes out of the Darkness, but blame yourself if you prefer the Darkness. Be thankful though that you have the freedom to choose, but understand that if it looks like everything is going wrong around you, the best you can do to help in retaining a balance again is to do the right thing for yourself and those around you. And I guess you can hope, or maybe even pray for the best.

God allows evil because he has no control over the darkness, he can only help us if we choose the Light instead of the Night. The Light and the darkness have both always been, and always will be, and humanity determines which will be stronger in their lives, and the lives of those around them.

"Either God is love and just because humanity has been given freewill; or God is wicked because with the freewill he gives comes the choice to do evil, from which comes the consequence of pain and suffering. If God wants us to be free though, he cannot take away the choice to do what is wrong. For if we did not have the choice to do what is wrong then we would never really be free at all, hence we could never have a sense of accomplishment, or peace when we make the better choice. So in giving us freewill God is Love and Just, and he could never be defined as such in less there was hate and injustice existing opposite of God."

Light cannot have fellowship with Darkness, but one could not be without the other. Of course this could all just be a trick of logic, right?

Ignorance hinders progress, and till humanity learns common sense there will always be unbalance in the world... I judge a dangerous ideology, but I do not judge someone by their culture, religion, or race. I wondered why racism still exists throughout the world, for this hinders progress for humanity. I asked, 'why?' I sought after answers and I found them.

The Myth and Truth of Race - Time For the Other Side to the Story

Sometimes what people perceive as truth is in actuality a myth, and a myth brings up questions that cannot be answered, because they should never have to be asked. Religious people in particular have asked the question, "Where did black people come from?" And we can assume a Racist may ask the same question in a more negative context.

One idea that has surfaced comes from Genesis 4:15. After Cain killed Able the Bible says that Cain felt insecure about life and God said, "Therefore, whoever kills Cain, vengeance shall be taken on him sevenfold." and "the Lord set a mark on Cain, lest anyone finding him should kill him." Some have concluded that this "mark" was black skin. Others have said that Genesis 9:25; "Cursed be Canaan; a servant of servants he shall be to his brethren." (This was a curse Noah placed on Canaan for his father Ham's lack of respect.) It's been suggested that the people of Africa can trace their ancestry back to Ham, the apparent conclusion being that the black race has been in slavery more than any race in human history; therefore, it is concluded that this curse was genetically followed into Ham's offspring. This curse however was placed on Canaan, not Ham. Canaan's descendants were the Canaanites and they dwelt in what is now modern Israel (Genesis 9:15-19). Now let's see the evidence against both these theories.

The question, "Where did black people come from," is not valid, based on scientific discoveries. In fact the question should be, "Where did people with blue eyes and blond hair come from?" A question like this has an answer, for a question like this is not rooted in a myth. Friends', this is an attempt to explain to you the genetic mutation that is the white, blond haired, blue eyed people. This is not a racial issue; this is about bringing to light some facts that may cause only a Racist or perhaps a religious extremist to be uncomfortable. This is about truth, and the question is not being brought up so as to encourage any kind of hate.

Scientists agree that the only race with an eye color other than brown is of Caucasian decent from somewhere in their blood line. According to new research people with blue eyes have a single, common ancestor. "Originally, we all had brown eyes," says Hans Eiberg from the Department of Cellular and Molecular Medicine at the University of Copenhagen. A single individual not only caused the mutation of blue eyed people, but the mutation of the Caucasian race. A team of scientists tracked down the genetic mutation which they say occurred between six thousand and ten thousand years ago. They say the mutation affected the OCA2 gene, which is involved in the production of the pigment that gives color to our hair, skin and eyes called melanin. "A genetic mutation affecting the OCA2 gene in our chromosomes resulted in the creation of a 'switch,' which literally 'turned off' the ability to produce brown eyes," Eiberg says. The reduction of melanin in the iris of one's eyes dilutes brown eyes to blue.

Eiberg and his team examined the DNA from mitochondria, the cells energy making structures, of blue-eyed individuals in various different countries. Since the genetic material comes from females, it can trace maternal lineages. Segments of ancestral DNA are shuffled over the course of several generations, and the individuals have varying sequences. The segments that have not been reshuffled are called haplotypes, and if a group of individuals share long haplotypes, this means the sequence arose rather recently in our human ancestry.

"What they were able to show is that the people who have blue eyes in Denmark, as far as Jordan, these people all have this same haplotype, they all have exactly the same gene changes that are all linked to this one mutation that makes eyes blue," Hawks said in a telephone interview. "From this we can conclude that all blue-eyed individuals are linked to the same ancestor," Eiberg said. "They have all inherited the same switch at exactly the same spot in their DNA." In the January third online edition of the journal Human Genetics Eiberg and his colleagues detailed their study.

This genetic switch somehow spread throughout the world, and the mystery still remains on how we come from a time not too long ago when everyone on Earth had brown eyes, and (because of an increased amount of melanin in the body), everyone had darker skin, to the present where twenty to forty percent of the population has blue eyes, blond hair and lighter skin tone.

Is it not interesting that Adolf Hitler was under the impression that blue eyes, blond hair, and white skin were attributes to the ultimate race? This is an interesting question because scientists have discovered that individuals with lighter iris color have a higher prevalence of age-related macular degeneration (ARMD) and an increased risk of ARMD progression than those with darker iris color. Also there is an increased risk of unveal melanoma in people with blue or gray iris color. The "weakest nations", Hitler said, were those of "impure" or "mongrel races." Well what he considered to be the ultimate race was descended from a genetic mutation no more than ten thousand years ago. If what Hitler says about the weakest nations is true, then this would surely not apply to those of African descent, for they are as pure blood as it gets. If what some religious people claim about a genetic curse or a mark on Cain is true, then this curse or mark would more likely be the white skin and lighter colored eyes, and without a doubt it would not be black skin and brown eyes, since people with black skin and brown eyes have always been around since human beings walked the Earth.

This subject which has just been addressed may now be an issue to some of you, but hopefully some of you who didn't care before, are starting to. We all care about the truth, this is a certainty. If we don't care about the truth, and share the truth with others then we are being selfish, and should be held responsible for the ignorance of those around us. There are two sides to every story, and we've heard the one side that was used for years, now the other side has just been presented to you with scientific backing. We care about the kind of truth that is indisputable and not based off of stories told by vicious dictators or religious extremists, this is a truth that surely can offer positive change to our world and is strongly encouraged to share with others.

Life is like a Charles Dickens novel; we're all connected in this story we call life...

Great Minds Unite With Greater Minds

Great minds unite with greater minds and the wise value their enemies... But to what avail?

One may wonder if humanity depends much on their instincts anymore, or if they recognize the need for others. An evolutionary ecologist who studies the causes and consequences of family-living in animals discovers why some species help each other raise their young while others go at it alone. One such scientist named Rubenstein was left with the following conclusion after his research, "If you can't count on the rain coming when it's supposed to, thus producing the food you will need for yourself and your young, you're going to need a lot of help from other members of your family." (*One of the first great cities discovered through archeology comes to mind; city-state Ur in ancient Sumer. The people there lived in a land constantly affected by the elements; floods or dry spells, and these tough conditions helped them evolve intellectually faster. Seems as though when people are too comfortable, or life becomes too easy the random bursts of human insight decrease and the need for others becomes less.*) The causes and consequences of family-living in humans are no different than their animal counterparts at the core, although in recent years one may wonder if humanity is losing their primal instinct to survive.

Greatness begets more greatness, and no one can advance very far alone. So, even if someone is only out for themselves they better include others in their plans. After thorough research Rubenstein discovered, "Everyone's looking out for their own best interest," he said."If you breed on your own you will be producing offspring that are more related to you than if you are helping someone else. But if you can't go it alone, you can pass on at least a share of your genes by helping to raise relatives." In the savanna, where rain and food is less predictable, a *smart* starling chooses to maintain a close relationship with its kin to ensure propagation of the family lineage.

When studying history one can't help but notice valuable connections among the great people who fill the books; paths crossed which brought about life changing events. An example of a Great Mind who crossed paths with other greats is Mark Twain, and he is one of many.

If not for **Mark Twain** and the others he crossed paths with, would we have ever heard of Helen Keller?

Mark Twain was an American author and humorist, most noted for his novels, *The Adventures of Tom Sawyer* (1876), and its sequel, *Adventures of Huckleberry Finn* (1885),which was labeled as "the Great American Novel. Twain was called the "greatest American humorist of his age," and William Faulkner called him "the father of American literature." Twain moved to San Francisco, California in 1864, and as a journalist there he met writers such as Bret Harte, Artemus Ward, and Dan DeQuille. The young poet Ina Coolbrith and he shared a romance. Upon making friends with these notable writers he had his first success as a writer one year later with his humorous tall tale, "The Celebrated Jumping Frog of Calaveras County." This book brought him national attention. A couple years later Twain married a woman, from a wealthy and liberal family, named Olivia Langdon. Through his wife he met abolitionists, "socialists, principled atheists and activists for women's rights and social equality," including Harriet Beecher Stowe (his next-door neighbor), Frederick Douglass, and the writer and utopian socialist William Dean Howells, who became a long-time friend. Whether intentionally or not Twain seemed to draw great people towards him like a magnet, perhaps if not for these people he would have never been great at all.

Mark Twain was fascinated with science and scientific inquiry. He developed a close and lasting friendship with Nikola Tesla, (an inventor, physicist, and electro-mechanical engineer, who was known as "The Wizard of the West." He was instrumental in developing AC networks, and invented the radio.) The two great minds spent much time together in Tesla's laboratory. Twain had three inventions patented while in close relation with Tesla, the most commercially successful one was a self-pasting scrapbook; a dried adhesive on the pages only needed to be moistened before use. We can assume Twain was inspired by Tesla. *A Connecticut Yankee in King Arthur's Court* features a time traveler from America of that time, who uses his knowledge of science to introduce modern technology to Arthurian England. Twain was inspired to write this type of storyline after spending significant time with Tesla. The idea of alternate history presented in this book would later become a common feature of a science fiction sub-genre.

Thomas Edison, (an *inventor who was involved in some of the greatest inventions and technological developments in history*), visited Twain at his home in Connecticut and decided to film him. The footage was used in *The Prince and the Pauper* (1909), a two-reel short film. Thomas Edison was a man who had history with Nikolas Tesla prior to being acquainted with Twain. When Tesla first arrived in the United States, in New York he had a letter of recommendation from Charles Batchelor, a former employer and close associate to Edison. In the letter of recommendation to Thomas Edison, it is claimed that Batchelor wrote, 'I know two great men and you are one of them; the other is this young man.' Edison hired Tesla to work for his *Edison Machine Works*. Tesla's work began with simple electrical engineering and quickly progressed to solving some of the company's most difficult problems. He was even offered the task of completely redesigning the Edison Company's direct current generators. Tesla was destined to become rivals with Edison.

The bad blood between the two brilliant men started when "Edison accused Tesla of being ignorant of American Humor."Edison offered him $50,000 (~ US$1.1 million in 2007) for redesigning Edison's inefficient motor and generators, and making an improvement in both service and economy." When Tesla inquired about the payment for his work, Edison broke his word and replied with, "Tesla, you don't understand our American humor." Earning just eighteen dollars per week, Tesla would have had to work for 53 years to earn the amount promised to him. (The offer was equal to the initial capital of the company.) Needless to say Tesla resigned when he was refused a raise to twenty five dollars per week. He eventually found himself digging ditches for a short period of time, ironically for the Edison Company. Despite Edison's claim Tesla likely did understand American humor, because his eventual good friend Mark Twain was the forerunner to stand-up comedy.

While Mark Twain was a positive person with an ostentatious sense of humor, he was in severe debt off and on during his life. At one point he credited Henry H. Rogers, a Standard Oil executive, with saving him from financial ruin, their close friendship in later years was mutually beneficial. The Rogers became a surrogate family for Twain after he suffered a personal loss. The two men introduced each other to their acquaintances, one of whom Twain especially admired; the remarkable deaf and blind girl Helen Keller and her governess Anne Sullivan. Twain is credited for labeling Sullivan the "the miracle worker". Twain introduced these two to Henry H. Rogers, who with his wife paid for Keller's education at Radcliffe College. Later William Gibson's play and film adaptation was named after Twains label of Sullivan; *The Miracle Worker*. Twain also introduced Rogers to journalist Ida M. Tarbell, who interviewed him for a muckraking expose that led indirectly to the breakup of the Standard Oil Trust. On cruises aboard the *Kanawha*, Twain and Rogers were joined at frequent intervals by Booker T. Washington, the famed former slave who had become a leading educator. With a friend like Rogers, Twain met many other great people. Down the many paths of inspiration one of the last ones led him to Helen Keller. Despite her apparent disadvantages, physically and financially, the young Keller pursued her *vision* in life. She benefited from Twain's support during her college education and publishing. She was the first deaf and blind person to earn a Bachelor of Arts degree in 1904, at the age of 24.

If not for **Jules Gabriel Verne** and the great minds he came across, would we have heard of space flight so soon in our history?

In showing how the connections to Verne began let's start with him as a young day dreaming student to the French inventor Brutus de Villeroi. Villeroi was a professor of drawing and mathematics in 1842. Brutus later became famous for creating the US Navy's first submarine, the USS *Alligator*. A logical assumption would be that De Villeroi inspired the imaginative Verne's conceptual design for the Nautilus in *Twenty Thousand Leagues Under the Sea*. His father discovered he was slacking in his studies; writing his own little short stories instead of paying attention in class. He stopped financing his sons' education and at this point Verne was forced to support himself. While finding work as a stockbroker, Verne hated his occupation, even though he was rather successful. During this period, he met Victor Hugo; (whose best-known works are the novels *Les Misérables* and *The Hunchback of Notre-Dame*), and Alexandre Dumas; (best known for his historical novels of high adventure *The Count of Monte Cristo*, and *The Three Musketeers);* these two authors offered Jules Gabriel Verne writing advice. When Verne crossed paths with these authors the circumstances seemed rather common place; he did not seek them out. He grew as a writer upon being inspired by his new friends, and triumphed as an author. His success as a writer led to another important connection years later with a man named Tsiolkovsky. After reading Verne's novel "From the Earth to the Moon, one of the future founding fathers of rocketry and astronautics Konstantin Tsiolkovsky refuted Verne's idea of using a cannon for space travel. He concluded, "A gun would have to be impossibly long. The gun in the story would subject the payload to about 22000 g of acceleration." However, Konstantin was nevertheless inspired by Jules Gabriel Verne's story and he went onto developing the theory of spaceflight.

If not for **H.G Wells** and the great minds he inspired, would we have ever heard of the Atom Bomb and Nuclear Warfare?

One of Wells earliest connections was in 1889–90 when he found a post as a teacher at Henley House School where he taught and admired A. A. Milne, the author of Winnie-the-Pooh. Another positive influence he had was on C. S. Lewis. In Lewis's novel *That Hideous Strength*, the character Jules is a caricature of Wells, and much of Lewis's science fiction was written both under the influence of Wells and as an antithesis to his work (or, as he said, an "exorcism" of the influence it had on him).In much of H.G Wells' science fiction radioactive decay plays a large role, and this leads to the more destructive influence he had on great minds. The book *The World Set Free* contains what is surely his most prophetic "hit". The novel revolves around "an (unspecified) invention that accelerates the process of radioactive decay, producing bombs that explode with no more than the force of an ordinary high explosive—but which "continue to explode" for days on end. "Nothing could have been more obvious to the people of the earlier twentieth century", he wrote, "than the rapidity with which war was becoming impossible

[but] they did not see it until the atomic bombs burst in their fumbling hands". Leó Szilárd acknowledged how Wells' book inspired him to theorize the nuclear chain reaction. He wrote the letter for Albert Einstein's signature which resulted in the Manhattan Project that built the atomic bomb.

There have been connections like the one between writers **John Ernst Steinbeck, Jr.;** the American writer who is widely known for the Pulitzer Prize-winning novel *The Grapes of Wrath*, and his close associate, playwright Arthur Miller. **Ernest Miller Hemingway;** was an American author and journalist who had crossed paths with several great minds also. While working in Chicago as an associate editor of the monthly journal *Cooperative Commonwealth*, he met Sherwood Anderson; (an American novelist and short story writer, who's most enduring work is the short story sequence *Winesburg, Ohio)*. Other writers Anderson had influenced other than Hemingway, were William Faulkner, J. D. Salinger, Amos Oz, and also John Ernst Steinbeck Jr.

In Paris, Hemingway met writers Gertrude Stein, James Joyce and Ezra Pound for to whom he said "could help a young writer up the rungs of a career". Hemingway met influential painters such as Pablo Picasso, Joan Miró, and Juan Gris. All these acquaintances he had before writing his greatest novels, and being recognized in the mainstream. Hemingway met F. Scott Fitzgerald, and they formed a friendship of "admiration and hostility". Upon reading *The Great Gatsby* Hemingway was inspired, and decided his next work had to be a novel.

J.D Salinger met Hemmingway during World War Two in the campaign from Normandy into Germany where Hemmingway was working as a war correspondent. He had arranged to meet with him, for Hemmingway was a great influence to him. Salinger was impressed with Hemingway's friendliness and modesty, finding him more "soft" than his gruff public persona. Hemingway was impressed by Salinger's writing, and remarked: "Jesus, he has a helluva talent." The two writers began corresponding; Salinger wrote Hemingway in July 1946 that their talks were among his few positive memories of the war.

The great minds seem to be drawn to each other for better or worse, whether by coincidence or some kind of instinctual reason. They can lift up the next generation of thinkers, inspiring them to accomplish greater good, or they may motivate them into discovering more inventive ways of bringing destruction. At times life seems to be either a satire or a tragedy. Perhaps mankind's sparks of ingenuity bring about more trouble down the line than any positive outcome. They say "Birds of a feather flock together." The question is; are we heading towards a better future? Or are we ultimately destructive by nature, even when we don't try to be? Will our species be defined by our revolutionary thinkers in a positive light, or will we be defined by our addiction to self sabotage? Whether to a better future or our demise ... ultimately we will flock together."

Without evil, or an idea of all that is evil, freedom and thankfulness could not exist... Balance is the simple answer.

Necessary Evil

I will attempt to explain to you, and convince you of the necessity of hate, despair; evil in general. Hopefully you will be able to see that to love, or have hope is always the wiser choice in any situation.

Without evil, or an idea of all that is evil, freedom and thankfulness could not exist. I believe the reason for this is because opposites define each other. Death can define life, despair can define hope, desire defines hatred, destiny defines freedom, and yes darkness defines light.

As a credible example on how opposites define each other let us look at how despair defines hope. This is noticeable in the life of the holocaust survivor Simon Wiesenthal who wrote The Sunflower. When reading this moving and at times disturbing account, we see how Simon's clear perception of hope and forgiveness was defined by the misery that he endured in the Nazi prison camps. The key event in The Sun Flower is when an SS Member Nazi was on his deathbed, and he asked his nurse to bring a Jew to him. Simon was the one who came. To Simon's surprise the Nazi confessed all his horrible crimes to him and begged for forgiveness. The reason this was so surprising, is that the SS members were trained to believe that a Jews spirit was less than an animal, that they were subhuman, while the SS member was part of the ultimate race; in the same vein as comparing a Greek god to a subhuman. When asking for forgiveness from a Jew he was showing that he did not believe what he was trained to believe, and that the Jew was as human as he, and certainly not less than an animal.

Simon was on the brink of losing all hope and this Nazi gave him a new hope. Throughout the tortures that Simon still endures after this event, his hope grows as his despair increases, because he realizes that the Nazi's weren't just monsters as they appeared, but they were brainwashed humans who had lost all hope. And hope in eventual peace was all Simon had to hold on to, and without his feeling of despair for the Jew and Nazi alike, his new hope would be unattainable.

You too could choose to be hopeful when in despair, instead of hateful towards those who bring despair. Hate is what such perpetrators of despair feel empowered by, and hate is what we must avoid.

Now you will hear how other opposites define each other, and lastly you will see what these truths lead to, the summed up explanation on how evil or an idea of evil is necessary.

When thinking of human beings that have been classified as evil, Adolph Hitler comes to mind. When studying the life of Adolph Hitler you see the obvious and that is that he desired power and prosperity for his nation, his people the Germans. The reason his passion, and wants for his people turned to a strong hate towards the other races of the world is because of what happened after WWI in the Versailles Treaty; where all the nations were to come to an agreement on how everything would be summed up, so that there would never be another World War. Now I am not going to give you a detailed history lesson on how WWI begot WWII, but I will say that it was evident Germany got the bad deal at this treaty, in fact there nation was raped, and they were blamed for much of the First World War. They were left ruined while the other nations ganged up on them, and offered little if any help. The nation with the most fatherless children was in Germany during this time, and the young men grew up desperate for a Father figure. Adolph Hitler grew up angry and bitter towards the nations of the world, especially the Jews who were the wealthiest. He became the Father figure that his nation felt they needed, for he had determination and his desire was truly fueled by his hate, and what the people saw was a desire for justice. If you allow your desires to be fueled by hate then you may meet the same fate as Hitler.

What about the destiny of the person who was repressed, or was treated unjustly and decides that hate is not what should fuel their desire for justice, and freedom? Could they still inspire a nation, through love, instead of anger and hate? Allow me to speak briefly of the Dr Reverend Martin Luther King Jr. Let us see how his destiny defined freedom, and how his death defined life.

I can't imagine being a young African American Man growing up in the time that Mr. King grew. I can't imagine not being allowed to use the same restroom as someone else because of the color of my skin, or not being allowed in some stores, or restaurants because of the color of my skin. I cannot imagine being despised simply because of the color of my skin, and I'm sorry but I can't imagine being forgiving, loving or even hopeful towards someone that hated me so. I can't imagine growing up as Dr. King.

What exactly inspired the love and greatness in this man, perhaps it was spiritual, and perhaps it was God. I don't know, but I do know that he lived his destiny, and he changed the world. He did what he felt he must do, and he was bold, and determined. He had a dream and that dream defined the reality that we live, or aspire to live today. His destiny, as I'm sure you see, defined freedom for the generations that followed his legacy. He knew that he risked his life by standing for what was good and true, but that was a risk he was willing to take, because he understood that if he was willing to die for justice, truth, or love then his death would define his life.

You see how at times despair defines hope, desire defines hatred, destiny defines freedom and death can define life. So does the darkness define the light? Is an idea of evil the reason for why we perceive freedom and thankfulness the way we do?

According to psychologists Nevitt Sanford and Craig Comstock in their 1971 anthology, "Evil is an actuality, whether or not we choose to deny it." Whatever leads to people suffering or social destructiveness is evil. In a sense evil is synonymous with "senseless violence." Importantly though that tendency which -- whether in oneself or others -- would inhibit personal growth and expansion, destroy or limit natural potentialities, restrict freedom, fragment or disintegrate the personality, and diminish the quality of interpersonal relationships is defined as evil. The point in mentioning this is that psychologically the concept of evil exists, not just religiously.

You've heard of Ying and Yang, the need for right and wrong, and light and dark. If you understand these-then you understand the need for balance. Without total opposites there could not be choice, and without choices there could not be freedom, so without freedom how could we perceive peace? The light without the darkness is an unbalanced and unrealistic perception, for how could beauty exist if there was no complete opposite to compare it to? Allow me to rephrase; Freedom and peace is what every human seeks, and desires more than anything. What is important for you to understand, when it comes to the freedom of choice is that if a person did not have the freedom to do what they are told not to do, or cannot do, then true freedom would be impossible to grasp. In addition to this, without freedom a lasting peace would be improbable. Thus the necessity of what is wrong or evil is required, because freedom could not be if you did not have the choice to do what is wrong. Am I going to have an affair, or be faithful? Am I going to lie, or tell the truth? Forgive, or hold a grudge? Love or hate? Right and wrong is choice.

Thankfulness would not exist without evil. I am thankful that I have a home and warm bed to sleep in, but if there was no possibility of me sleeping in the street, in the cold winter air, then I would not be thankful. I am thankful that I have the freedom to be a light in the darkness that is all around, if I so desire to be, but I as well as you need the darkness to shine through. I am thankful that I can have pride in myself when I choose to do what is right instead of what is wrong. I am thankful that history has proven time and time again that the way of hate brings chaos, while the way of love brings peace.

I hope I have swayed you into respecting the concept of hate, or evil and to understanding why love and hope is the wiser choice.

The philosopher Allen Moore was contemplating the importance of evil when he said; "Perhaps evil is the humus formed by virtues decay and perhaps it is from that dark, sinister loam that virtue grows strongest."

"People say they want the truth, but they usually don't mean it. The truth is the one thing most avoid in this narcissistically bred generation…"

The Successful Domestication of Man

A dog is usually happy with life and loyal to his or her Master, not even seeming to recognize their lack of freedom. The dog has been bred to serve man for thousands of years, and the Master takes the dog for granted. The dog expects the Master is watching, waiting to give praise, orders, or reprimand, and the dog is grateful. The dog doesn't know how to survive in Mans' world without him, for Man knows what's best, and he provides purpose. The Master is accepted with adoration, respect, and appreciation. For the dog the Master gives meaning to life, and for the dog ignorance is truly bliss.

What enslaves Humanity? What can people not live without? How can we be free? These questions are very important but for many the answers are not so simple.

"Sure must be a great consolation to the poor people who lost their stock in the late crash to know that it has fallen in the hands of Mr. Rockefeller, who will take care of it and see it has a good home and never be allowed to wander around unprotected again. There is one rule that works in every calamity. Be it pestilence, war, or famine, the rich get richer and poor get poorer. The poor even help arrange it."

By Will Rogers
Diary of America

If the poor can be guided in a particular direction, they can be trained to unknowingly provide the means of making the rich richer, and even be thankful for this. There was an evangelical preacher whose soul message was "money is good and God intended for all Christians to be rich", this was the message in a nut shell.

The preacher paced himself when delivering his message, and he even had intense music being played with which his preaching seemed to keep rhythm. By the end of the message he seemed to have everyone there convinced that the more money they brought up to the stage for him and his ministry the more money God would bless them with for giving out of the goodness of their hearts. People rushed to the stage and soon there were piles of cash at the preachers' feet. The whole process seemed so simple... How much more is this simple method applied to the masses on a far greater scale? A society full of sheep naturally entices the wolves. What this preacher did is being done by those who have been wealthy for generations. There are those who know the game quite well, and they have even made the rules for how the game is played. Those who do not know the rules of the game may live a happy life spent with family and friends. They openly accept the label of being middle class or blue collared as a stamp of honor, and they live faithful lives at times being thankful for what they do have.

"People will try to convince you of their beliefs and convictions because it reinforces their beliefs and convictions. If a belief and conviction needs something to reinforce it, then it can't stand on its own. Choose to remove erroneous beliefs and temper your convictions with facts and NOT supposition. Then, and only then, will you be able to understand Divine truth."

Professor Dean A. Banks

Some of the elite in society will try to convince us of certain beliefs and convictions which they do not believe in. They will do this so as to reinforce their agenda. If they can persuade you into seeing things in the way they want you to, then you can be led by them willingly and unknowingly. By habit, or ritual people are more likely to listen to what the wealthy have to say before they'll listen to someone who is poor or middle class; because of this mindset certain beliefs are allowed to form which shouldn't be able to stand. The fact that we cannot survive right now and provide for a family without oil, electricity, and plenty of money is the evidence in how the wealthy control the masses. "If we choose to remove erroneous beliefs and temper our convictions with facts and not supposition, then, and only then, will we be able to understand Divine truth."

To solve any problem or to discover the cause, the proven method is to go to the foundation of the quandary. What commodity do people feel they need much of today, which in reality we shouldn't need at all? Let's try looking back at the origin of the black gold rush, or more so those who started the significant expansion of the oil industry. The world's first billionaire was John Davison Rockefeller, America's most generous philanthropist. Rockefeller's wealth was based largely on the near global control of oil refining. It's documented and well known how he also had large interests in other monopolies. As the economist Anthony Sutton notes, Rockefeller "controlled the copper trust, the smelters trust and the gigantic tobacco trust, in addition to having influence in some Morgan properties such as the U.S. Steel Corporation as well as in hundreds of smaller industrial trusts, public service operations, railroads and banking institutions. National City Bank was the largest of the banks influenced by Standard Oil-Rockefeller, but financial control extended to the U.S. Trust Co. and Hanover National Bank [and] major life insurance companies - Equitable Life and Mutual of New York" (Wall Street and the Bolshevik Revolution, 1981). Johns' descendents are said to have been hardworking German immigrants, and his father, William Avery Rockefeller, was a travelling salesman, rumored to have excelled as a con man. He sold bogus products to the sick and desperate, being able to convince many to buy expensive remedies that were either useless or downright dangerous. "He would be gone for months and come back with a great roll of money.... He would go to small towns advertising himself as 'The Celebrated Dr. Levingston.' William announced he could cure anything, but made a specialty of cancer and kidney troubles." (MacDonald, "Double Life," New York World, February 2, 1908). John Rockefeller, learned all he needed to from his father, and he dropped out of high school in 1855 to take a business course. John was motivated and soon he was ready to take on the world.

John watched the trends, recognizing the predictability and gullibility of humanity. He was inspired by what he saw, and his vision was forming; a vast vision which seemed to have no limit. The Civil War compelled him into the oil business in 1863. John along with others from wealthy families, like J.P. Morgan- paid $300 to avoid conscription; a small price to pay, while thousands less fortunate died in the war. (Of course this is one of the rules to the game though; the wealthy make wars, or supports them, and they benefit financially while the young and poor die fighting for what they view as a just cause. Like a loyal servant to his or her Master, many brave people die for a lie.) John sold whiskey at inflated rates to Federal soldiers during the onset of the war. He invested his profits into oil refineries next. The South was supplying turpentine to the North for camphene- fueled lights. When the war cut off the North's access to this fuel, kerosene from Pennsylvania oil quickly took over as the lamp fuel of choice and stimulated Johns' oil business... John was young, but he knew the rules of the game, he was able to control people and situations to his advantage.

John and a few partners organized The Standard Oil Company in 1870, with capital of $1 million dollars. This company was built through him 'buying out competitors, price cutting and controlling secondary businesses related to pipelines, trains, oil terminals and barrel making.' By 1880, his monopoly controlled the refining of 95% of America's oil. In a few years 70% of Standard Oil's sales were overseas, largely to northern Europe and Russia. The properties were merged into the Standard Oil Trust with an initial capitalization of $70 million, and by 1900 Rockefeller controlled about two-thirds of the entire world's oil supply. John was also a director of the U.S. Steel Corp when it formed in 1901. John used a commodity like oil to conquer the world; he helped make dead dinosaur ooze into a valued product which people would fight for and invest millions into.

Many people looked up to John Rockefeller, many admired him and saw him as a generous person, and many felt they needed him in their lives. He knew what the world needed, or so this is what many believed. He cared for the betterment of humanity, and was one of the most generous philanthropists the world has known. He provided thousands with jobs, eventually millions, and he provided oil to all who needed this. Eventually people were more dependent on oil than any other commodity. After a few generations the habit was ingrained into humanity, almost to the point where one might say they seemed to need oil, (and what oil provided), as much as one needed water.

Was in 1911, the U.S. Supreme Court had Rockefellers' monopoly dissolved into about three dozen companies. Many of these oil companies are household names today like Chevron (Standard Oil California), Amoco (Standard Oil Indiana), Mobil (Standard Oil New Jersey) and Exxon, (Standard Oil New Jersey). Rockefeller still profited from this change and the loss of his monopoly, and his decedents still profit today. Today oil is the number one source of profit for the most wealthy and elite in society. Even though we have the technological means of running vehicles and other machines on something other than fossil fuel we do not. In the year 2012 humans still rely on oil, but the only reason this is still the case is because the rich are not ready for change, not as long as they still profit.

People are bred to feed the greed of a select few; we were domesticated thousands of years ago. Before the rise of the Rockefeller dynasty and the prevailing commodity of oil there were others like John Rockefeller, those who used the rules of the game to change the way the masses reasoned. They planted the seeds of persuasion, which grew from generation to generation. The game had been used before with bronze, silver, gold, and other precious stones and minerals, where even the Ages of man were defined by the reining commodity of the time. The idea of these commodities being of immense value and greatly desired was a seed planted by the Masters, something the wolves used to enslave humanity.

The wild is free, and the wild is balanced. Back in the days when we were walking alongside other humanoids like Neanderthal and Homo-Erectus, we were aggressive creatures, but physically and intellectually superior to modern day humans. Although we were struggling to survive in a harsh environment and times could be hard, we were free... Today we're more like dogs.

The Dog is a different creature today than his ancestors were over forty thousand years ago. You can see this by looking at the modern Gray Wolf, for based on genetic evidence this is the animal the dog once was. When the wolf was domesticated quite a few physical or morphological changes occurred. The most significant changes happened within only several generations; changes in coat coloration and markings, reduction in overall size, a shorter jaw initially with crowding of the teeth and the shrinking in size of the teeth; a reduction in brain size resulting in changes to cranial capacity (affecting the areas of the brain relating to alertness and sensory processing. The wolf, once becoming a tamed dog, had lost the skills necessary for survival in the wild).

A recent experiment done by the Russian Scientist Dmitry Belyaev has proven just how quickly an animal can evolve under the right circumstances. His research and methods have helped us better understand the domestication of our most loyal servant, the dog. Dmitry wanted to reenact how domestication may have occurred and he did this through the "farm fox" experiment. Wild silver foxes were selectively bred for forty years and the result was more dog-like animals that were friendly towards humans. The domestic elite foxes actually sought out human attention and indulged in human affection after only a human generation. The most fascinating observation by Dmitry Belyaev was the change in physical traits which paralleled the selection for tameness, even though the physical traits were not originally selected for. The once wild silver foxes were giving birth to foxes with floppy ears, spotted or black-and-white coats, tails that curled, and even the barking vocalization and earlier sexual maturity was noticeable; the silver fox was literally turning into a dog.

It was reported by those involved in the experiment, "On average, the domestic foxes respond to sounds two days earlier and open their eyes one day earlier than their non-domesticated cousins. More striking is that their socialization period has greatly increased. Instead of developing a fear response at 6 weeks of age, the domesticated foxes don't show it until 9 weeks of age or later. The whimpering and tail wagging is a holdover from puppyhood, as are the foreshortened face and muzzle. Even the new coat colors can be explained by the altered timing of development. One researcher found that the migration of certain malanocytes (which determine color) was delayed, resulting in a black and white 'star' pattern." The wild was bred out of the silver fox in such a short time, and the physical changes show a far more vulnerable looking creature; an animal dependent on humanity.

The Cro-Magnon man was different than the modern day man, he even looked different, and like the farm fox in the experiment Man started out wild and free. Cro-Magnon had more meat on his bones; he had broader shoulders and massive muscles. As a general rule science says to control massive muscle blocks, the more brain you need. This may also be partially why the burly Neanderthal had larger brains than modern day Homo-Sapiens. Twenty thousand to thirty thousand years ago the Homo-Sapiens with the biggest brains lived; with his broad chest, larger teeth and strong jaws, Cro-Magnon Man was also brilliant. "Recent studies of human fossils suggest the brain shrank more quickly than the body in near-modern times." Scientists discovered that as the human population rose and societies became more complex the brain started to shrink. When humans didn't have to be as smart to stay alive and they could depend on others supplies to provide for them; their intelligence decreased. The Cro-Magnon man became the Homo-Sapiens we are today because we've domesticated ourselves, according to Richard Wrangham, a primatologist at Harvard University. He notes on how every domesticated animal has lost about ten to fifteen percent of brain volume when compared with their wild progenitors. Wrangham also points out the physical changes. Homo-Sapiens today have slighter builds than the Cro-Magnon, as well as smaller teeth, and smoother faces; equivalent of the floppy ears and curled tails on the transformed foxes or gray wolves. The humans who live today have had much of the aggression from the wild bred out of them, leaving us more susceptible to others ruling over us. Today the modern man depends on the wealthier, thus supposed more intelligent individuals to rule over us, instead of the larger and strongest of humans like in ancient times. Ironically the bigger and stronger Cro-Magnon was probably more intelligent than those we consider wise today. What many people today don't realize though is that the wealthiest people today are not always the more intelligent; they simply follow the simple rules to a game which has been passed down to them by their wealthy elders. They rely on the fact that ultimately people today are stupid, and usually not too aggressive to be deemed as threatening.

"The story written in our bones is that we look more and more peaceful over the last 50,000 years," Wrangham says. And that is not all. If he is correct, domestication has also transformed our cognitive style. His hunch is based on studies-many done by his former graduate student Brian Hare-"comparing domestic animals with their wild relatives."

The wealthy elite may have been using the rules to the game passed down for generations but they are not of superior intellect and the evidence is there to be seen. Just looking at our present economy and our nations rising deficit, this shows how those who rule over the masses have a flawed system in place. Those of elite status who ruled over humanity in Roman times they also showed how their system was flawed, as the world fell into the Dark Ages. History is about to repeat herself once again.

In Utah the NSA (National Security Agency) is constructing a data center unlike any other. The purpose is "to intercept, decipher, analyze, and store vast swaths of the world's communications sent down through satellites and through the underground and undersea cables of international, foreign, and domestic networks. The heavily fortified $2 billion center is scheduled to be running in September 2013." Flowing through its servers and routers will be all forms of communication, including "the complete contents of private emails, cell phone calls, and Google searches, as well as all sorts of personal data trails-parking receipts, travel itineraries, bookstore purchases, and other personal information from billions will be stored in these near-bottomless databases."

"In the process-and for the first time since Watergate and the other scandals of the Nixon administration-the NSA has turned its surveillance apparatus on the US and its citizens. It has established listening posts throughout the nation to collect and look through billions of email messages and phone calls, whether they originate within the country or overseas. It has created a supercomputer of almost unimaginable speed to look for patterns and unscramble codes. Finally, the agency has begun building a place to store all the trillions of words and thoughts and whispers captured in its electronic net." James Bamford (Wired magazine)

Why do we allow this invasion of our privacy? This leach from the NSA is obviously destined to drain what's left of our presumed freedom in America. We are living in a time where humanity accepts such an obvious invasion of privacy and a precursor to the complete visual loss of our freedom. We allow this because the data center is supposed to protect us from future cyber attacks and other terrorist threats. "Some of the elite in society will try to convince us of certain beliefs and convictions... They will do this so as to reinforce their agenda." They feel no guilt in this; simply survival of the fittest. Their agenda is to stay in power and keep the masses feeding the rich. When people live in fear and they grow in ignorance they will desperately trust in those who have power over them. Much of the time we depend on the knowledge of others and their technology for survival in this day, instead of thinking for ourselves. So we'll accept the invasion of privacy, and we will trust those over us, because after all we're not really free today. Ultimately we'll place our trust in the wealthy elite, even though we'll gripe and complain we will depend on our Masters. We will turn to those whom are supposed to have our best interest in mind, because we've been bred to. How many times are we going to insanely stand by as the wealthy elite claim the foul smelling bitter fluid flowing over us is rain? The answer is, time and time again, even till the last of our freedom is taken away.

Some people have the dream of being like the wealthy elite, they dream of being higher on the food chain. So many people go into credit debt, and lose thousands while pretending to be more like the Masters they so admire. People have become creatures of habit and the way we have been living for several generations has proven to be self destructive. Eventually even the wealthy elite will not benefit any longer from the ignorance of man. Thousands die in wars fought in vain, wars which last for years, and only the wealthy truly benefit. People still live for the prearranged dream though, believing wealth buys happiness and peace of mind. They're unable to recognize how all of the material possessions, their dependence on the prized commodity of oil, and the wasted desperate desire of these keeps humanity enslaved.

A man or woman is usually happy with life and loyal to their Master, not even seeming to recognize their lack of freedom. They've been bred to serve a select few over them. They help the Master grow in wealth, being satisfied with the scraps thrown to them from the feast. Humanity expects the Master is watching, waiting to give praise, orders, or reprimand, and we are grateful. We don't know how to survive in the present world without the wealthy elite. We need others in power over us. We accept the Master with adoration, respect, and appreciation. For the dog the Master gives meaning to life, and for the dog ignorance is truly bliss.

Just a man showing his appreciation for the one he loves when comparing his time with her to the wonders he has seen throughout his life… there is hope....

My Muse

The life I had before the life I have now contained moments so wonderful, so seamless, that they will always be worthy of reflection. And I'm sure you had such moments as well, that you find so worthy of remembrance.

I remember seeing the blood red sun set over the shimmering blue ocean in Acapulco, while I was lying in the warm water so comfortably. Absolute relaxation overcame me, and everything seemed so peaceful.

I remember climbing to the top of an immense waterfall in Yosemite and staring out at the endless sea of lustrous green trees as far as my eyes could see. I felt like I was in another realm; as if where I stood were Paradise.

I remember watching the ancient sun rise in the vast desert of Kirkuk. The sun was appearing like I have never seen it before, bringing incomparable beauty to such a loathsome and barren wasteland.

I remember holding my daughter in my hands for the first time, being so grateful over how perfect she looked. My own little Cherub staring up into my eyes, words could never describe the beauty I saw in those moments.

These were all times that were wonderful and serene for me. When I look back on those moments, I feel like there was not something missing, but someone. Someone I wish I could have shared all these superlative moments with, not just someone like you, but you.

We will see wonders together to add to our past moments of clarity. We will live our new life in novel beauty, and unfolding new mysteries together. Seeing our share of sunsets, finding our own paradise, and bringing beauty into places where the land seems so barren and ugly. We will not only be like a rising sun in each other's eyes, but our love will shine for others.

And when we bring life into this world together we will be witness to a beauty that words cannot express, but only you and I will understand.

The life we had has prepared us for the life we have. And even back then, through seamless moments so worthy of remembrance, I believe I was waiting and hoping for the moments we share now.

I'm suffering with misanthropy as of late, yet the military doctors' prognosis is PTSD (Post Traumatic Stress Disorder). I need to escape society! I need to detox in an attempt at trying to hold onto hope, for I see us drowning in ignorance. People don't want to see, and they don't want the truth, yet they lie to themselves and claim they do. People want to live in a false reality, and they have the audacity to be surprised when tragedies occur which could have been avoided if they paid attention to the obvious warnings. After returning from Afghanistan my hate for humanity has increased. My frustration over our obsession with self-destruction increases daily. If the people don't care then why should I care? Why should I continue to share with them the truths, if they don't care to read them anyway? My respect for any person is limited, and truth be told my love seems only for my wife and children these days...How do I escape the burning city?

The Truth of Humanity We Don't Want To See

The evidence is there; **"authority clouds people's ethical judgment,"** and if they are not so easily intimidated they may be easier brainwashed. People are prone to obeying authority even if what is asked of them is clearly morally wrong. Since many are looking for someone else to tell them the way they are vulnerable to allowing the manipulation of their minds.

In 1966 Psychiatrist Charles Hofling described an experimental protocol. (What was especially sad about this experiment is that those involved were not brainwashed victims, but they understood the choice they were making as well as the potential consequence.)

The experimental procedures were explained to a group of twelve nurses and twenty-one nursing students. The experiment would involve an unknown doctor calling real nurses on the hospital's night shift and asking them to administer twice the maximum dose of an unapproved drug to a patient. Unbeknown to the nurses, the "medicine" was actually a harmless sugar pill and the doctor was a fake.

They were asked to predict how many nurses, would give an overdose of a drug to the patient. Out of the twelve nurses, ten said they wouldn't do it. Out of the nursing students all twenty-one said they'd refuse to administer the drug.

When Dr. Hofling actually tried the experiment 22 nurses at a hospital in the United States were chosen. "They were each called by an experimenter with the alias of Dr. Smith who said that he would be around to write up the paperwork as soon as he got to the hospital." The nurses were stopped at the door to the patient's room before they could administer the "drug".

Dr. Hofling discovered that 21 out of the 22 nurses would have given the patient an overdose of medicine. None of the investigators, and only one experienced nurse who examined the protocol in advance, correctly guessed the experimental results. He also found that all 22 nurses whom he had given the questionnaire to had said they would not obey the orders of the doctor, and that 10 out of the 22 nurses had done this before, with a different drug. The researchers clearly labeled the drug, so nurses knew they were overdosing their patients. The nurses also violated hospital rules by taking instructions over the phone and giving an unapproved medicine. With results like this it's a wonder many would be surprised at all.

The nurses were thought to have allowed themselves to be deceived because of their high opinions of the standards of the medical profession. "The study revealed the danger to patients that existed because the nurses' view of professional standards induced them to suppress their good judgment."

More troubling news is the evidence of how easily people can be brainwashed, something which has been proven on the largest of scales. In America **the Jonestown Massacre comes to mind, where the death toll was 918 people; most deadly single non-natural disaster in U.S. history until September 11, 2001.** Nazi Germany comes to mind when it comes to examples in history where millions seem to be brainwashed.

In the 1950s, the CIA launched a top-secret program called MKULTRA. The purpose of this was to discover any possible means to use in controlling people's minds.

"For two decades, the CIA used hallucinogens, sleep deprivation and electrical shock techniques in their endeavor at perfecting brainwashing."

CIA scientists conducted hundreds of research projects as part of MKULTRA. One project involved testing the effects of LSD in public by slipping the drug to unaware bar patrons in New York and San Francisco.

In 1973 CIA Director Richard Helms ordered documents related to the project destroyed, in fear over the outcome of the Watergate scandal. Some documents escaped destruction. In 1977 a Freedom of Information Act request released more than 20,000 pages on the sordid program to author John Marks.

The truth of humanity we don't want to see is if people are not so easily intimidated they may be easier brainwashed. People are prone to obeying authority, even if what is asked of them is clearly morally wrong. And since many are looking for someone else to tell them the way, instead of trusting their intuition, many are vulnerable to allowing the manipulation of their minds.

Emotions

Emotions drive humanity and can destroy humanity.

Emotions define our nature and are the reason behind destructive patterns.

Those with presence of mind persuade humanity and can save humanity.

Those with presence of mind can use ones emotions against them like a rope tied around their neck used to guide them.

Emotions can make us vulnerable and weak.

Emotions can make us act hasty and foolishly.

Presence of mind makes us aware of our vulnerabilities and provides us with the courage to overcome our weakness.

Presence of mind offers the ability to use ones enemy's emotions against them like a rope, for as they act in a hasty and foolish manner; they tighten their rope around their neck and then hang themselves.

Emotions drive humanity and can destroy humanity.

Those with presence of mind persuade humanity and can save humanity.

Is there hope?

I have seen there is purpose, so there must be hope.

Although the path looks strange and the terrain uneven... if this is the path to true freedom then what better journey could I take? Surely the way the multitudes follow down is not leading us anywhere worth going... Debts grow, greed grows, our enemies increase, and ignorance does as well. The Rat Race is masked slavery and when we remain in the race we cannot live a truly honest life. True Freedom; is not having to depend on the illusion that money and power will someday buy you happiness and freedom. The wealthy politicians are meant to be the biggest servants for those in their nation; they just do a really lousy job at this because they forget their place and we don't fire them for their incompetence... Let the world call me crazy, while I choose freedom instead of the illusion that I must depend on monopoly money for happiness and be concerned about the invisible ceiling of debt which expands to trillions of dollars... Call me insane (because I want to stop making the same mistakes humanity has been making over and over again.) I will sell my house and all the garbage I don't need; (T.V, Stereo, furniture, old comic books, movies, etc.), buy my cheap land along with the mineral rights and put my TSP savings in an account accessible.... Let the rest of the world continue playing pretend as if they're heading towards some worthwhile prize, "as for me and my house we will not serve the lies of this present world any longer." Now if for some reason this does not work out, then I will share the truth with you; that there is not true freedom in this world, but just an illusion. However if my vision does work out I will share the hard truths with you whether you want to hear them or not. You may ask "why?"... Because I still care.

When we were children we had dreams, we had hope. As we grew older we lost something significant, something magical... actually we didn't lose this, it was taken from us. Our only hope for the future is our children, and I will not allow them to be taken from, I will provide them with a better way.

- *Basic Psychiatric Concepts in Nursing* (1960). Charles K. Hofling, Madeleine M. Leininger, Elizabeth Bregg. J. B. Lippencott, 2nd ed. 1967: ISBN 0-397-54062-0
- *Textbook of Psychiatry for Medical Practice* edited by C. K. Hofling. J. B. Lippencott, 3rd ed. 1975: ISBN 0-397-52070-0
- *Aging: The Process and the People* (1978). Usdin, Gene & Charles K. Hofling, editors. American College of Psychiatrists. New York: Brunner/Mazel Publishers
- *The Family: Evaluation and Treatment* (1980). ed. C. K. Hofling and J. M. Lewis, New York: Brunner/Mazel Publishers
- *Law and Ethics in the Practice of Psychiatry* (1981). New York: Brunner/Mazel Publishers, ISBN 0-87630-250-9
- *Custer and the Little Big Horn: A Psychobiographical Inquiry* (1985). Wayne State University Press, ISBN 0-8143-1814-2
- http://en.wikipedia.org/wiki/MKULTRA

- http://en.wikipedia.org/wiki/File:DeclassifiedMKULTRA.jpg

www.ingramcontent.com/pod-product-compliance
Lightning Source LLC
Chambersburg PA
CBHW060408290526
45791CB00002B/664